# CAREERS IN MUSIC

American Music Conference

# CAREERS IN MUSIC

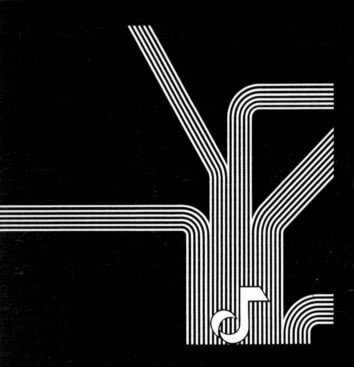

The publication of
CAREERS IN MUSIC
was made possible through
a special grant from
THE CBS FOUNDATION

Library of Congress Catalog Card Number 76-150-516

ISBN 0-918196-00-0

Printed in U.S.A.

music

# FOREWORD

## Choosing A Career

To the thousands upon thousands of people working in it, the music business isn't a business at all. It's fun, fulfilling and a wonderfully satisfying way of earning a living. Most wouldn't trade music for any other field.

Of course there are frustrations and disappointments as in any other job area. But the personal rewards in music for the performer, educator, retailer and manufacturer are very great indeed.

Is a career in music for you? That's a big question you'll be asking yourself as you read this book. And we've tried to be candid. We hope you'll be honest with yourself in assessing your own personal qualities and talents realistically.

Performing careers (whether in the classical or popular field) are the most visible. They are also the most demanding, the most competitive and have the fewest opportunities for beginners.

There are, however, literally dozens of other career possibilities in music—some of which you may never have considered. We hope these pages will expand your own horizons about the many music-related jobs that require an understanding of music—but not necessarily either professional level performing skills or any performing ability at all.

Success in any facet of music—as in any other career—requires determination, diligence, energy, dedication and a measure of luck. Don't be blinded by glamour. Movies and TV dramas rarely show the long years of hard work which most often lead to the "instant success."

While we have reviewed a number of career areas, we have not been able to include the almost endless variation in each. Numerically, there are probably more jobs in aspects of music education. However, the music business is a "growth industry" because of the tremendous national interest in active music participation. And that means new job possibilities spring up with each technological advance, new teaching technique, new marketing idea.

2

At the end of the book we have listed sources for additional information. You may want to write these associations, as well as check with your school guidance counselor, the dean of the music school at your state college or university, or anyone you know in the career area you'd like to consider entering.

Your school or public library will probably also have available many of the trade publications in the music field. By reading them you'll get even more of the flavor of the profession.

Even if you eventually decide on a job outside the music industry remember that music study and participation are their own rewards. Learning how to play an instrument helps to develop skills and understanding that will pay you handsome personal dividends regardless of what career you finally do select. Playing a musical instrument is a great source of enjoyment throughout life—which is why America has so many millions of amateur musicians.

None of our advice is meant to discourage you, only to arm you with sufficient information to let you know what you can expect in the music business. If you have the talent, the determination and the perseverance to work toward your goal, you can succeed. There's room in the music industry for everyone who really wants to "make it." We hope you do.

**The American Music Conference**

**Betty Stearns**
**Clara Degen**
Editors

# TABLE OF CONTENTS

## Careers in Business

## Careers in the Recording Industry

Covers positions in *record production* including producer, arranger, copyist, union contractor, musician leader, studio performer and engineer / mixer. Includes a section on *the business side of recording* covering sales, merchandising, promotion, graphics, manufacturing and general management. Also reviews jobs for disc jockeys and music attorneys.

## Careers in Allied Fields

# PERFORMING ARTS

The information in the chapter which
follows was compiled with
the assistance of

SSgt. Frank Byrnes, U. S. Marine Corps Band

Martha E. Freitag, American
Symphony Orchestra League

Maj. Marvin E. Keefer, U.S. Army Bands

Dr. Mort Lindsey, conductor/
composer for television and films

Walter Wager, American Society of
Composers, Authors and Publishers [ASCAP]

# Careers in Popular Music

# Careers in Popular Music

Have you ever heard the story about the tourist who asked a New York cab driver how to get to Carnegie Hall and was told, "Practice, buddy, practice"? The joke may be old, but the advice is still sound—and it applies to performing careers in all areas of music, popular as well as symphonic.

If your dream is a career in popular music, be advised that the field is highly competitive. Even if you have the talent, success depends on a great deal of hard work and an even greater degree of luck. A sound musical education is essential.

Ask most performers who have made a name for themselves in popular music for advice on how to get started, and chances are you'll get a one-word answer: "Don't." They'll point out that no matter how glamorous life can be at the top, the road up gets pretty rocky and sometimes doesn't lead anywhere at all.

Ask them again, however, if they regret the struggle or would change their careers for anything and the reply is invariably: "No." Many musicians, like artists in other fields, perform because they feel they must—because music is where their aptitude lies. They *know* their talent is above average. They believe that they have something special to contribute to music or that they are good enough to make a living performing.

If that's your story, if you were born to perform and are sure you have a statement to make in the popular music idiom, the possibilities are many and varied. Rock, jazz, blues, country, folk, Latin, ethnic—any and all of these, plus classical music, mix and mingle in an astonishing number of ways to create the sounds of today.

You can perform solo or as part of a group. You can expect to play almost anywhere: in clubs, pubs, theaters, churches, schools, parks, at fairs and summer festivals. You might even find yourself in a television or motion picture studio, or working for a major record company.

And you could be playing almost any instrument. The piano, guitar, trombone, saxophone, trumpet, drums, etc., fit into most musical ensembles, but a mark can be made with anything from a harmonica to a sitar. The piano, violin and flute are being used by many rock groups to give "new" sounds to contemporary compositions.

Often an unusual combination of instruments gives performing groups a uniquely appealing sound. If you have mastered more than one instrument or if you sing as well as play an instrument, your chances for success are that much better.

If you play a keyboard instrument, do some experimenting with synthesizers. Some synthesizers are activated by keyboard-like controls and can be programmed to duplicate the sounds of familiar instruments or create totally new tonal effects.

In the late 60s, during what is already being called "The Golden Age of Rock," major record companies staged frantic talent hunts for new performers in the pop/rock field. Those days are gone, due in part to a glutted market and also because of huge increases in production and promotion costs.

## Getting Started

Beware the myth of overnight stardom. True, Cinderella stories do happen every now and then, but don't be discouraged if the "big break" doesn't come. Plan instead on becoming one of the large number of unsung musicians who make a good, steady income doing what they love and know best: making music. It is generally from the ranks of hard working musicians that the "instant sensations" come.

To get started, you need to establish a reputation—not with the general public, but among other musicians. That means going where other musicians can be found. Every sizeable city has a music community, but larger cities obviously offer more contacts and more opportunities.

The city you choose may depend in part on what kind of music you play or what your ultimate career goals are. Some cities are well known for particular styles of popular music, and so can provide unique training grounds for young musicians interested in that style. Nashville, of course, is the mecca of country and western musicians. Chicago gave birth to urban blues and is still one place to go to see masters of the genre in action. But you can find blues in Boston and country music in Seattle. Take advantage first of what's available close to home. Learn what you can, then move on. Experience is the key to success.

# Careers in Popular Music

If you've always wanted to work in television, your best bet is Los Angeles. New York, once a mecca for performers with aspirations for television work, is no longer a viable outlet for televised music. It is, however, still the major market for those with ambitions to produce jingles and commercials.

The recording industry is centered in Los Angeles, New York and Nashville, but important work is being done in other cities including Detroit, Chicago and Atlanta. The center for professional musical theater is still New York, but theaters are sprouting up all over. Again, investigate local possibilities first.

Most of the musicians who work in television, the theater, movies, or for recording studios these days are session musicians—hired on a per-job basis. Some television shows, "The Tonight Show" for example, do have a permanent orchestra or band, but that's becoming more and more of a rarity. Similarly, theaters and recording studios do not as a rule have house bands. When backup musicians are needed, they are drawn from the city's musical community.

In any city, therefore, the same musicians can be expected to turn up in any number of places. For example, a Chicago jazz trombonist leads his own band in a neighborhood club on Monday nights, plays in someone else's combo on Wednesday nights and backs a headliner in a supper club on weekends. While his evenings are devoted to live performances, his days are frequently spent in a recording studio cutting albums or taping television commercials.

This trombonist is a successful professional musician, but he doesn't do the same thing all the time. He survives in a tough profession by being good, versatile, reliable and by being able to read any piece of music that's put in front of him.

## Develop Skills, Versatility

To be able to do any kind of studio work, says award-winning conductor-composer Henry Mancini, "You have to be an excellent musician. There is simply no time for practice at home. Studio instrumentalists must be first-rate readers and extremely flexible. A sax man might have to play a musical comedy score in the morning and switch to a 'big dance' sound in the afternoon. Or he might have a record date for a country music album.

"When I record a film score, for example, the music is first seen by the musicians the day they're called. They have to read the score through with reasonable accuracy. Normally, with an easy piece, we can go for a take on the first run-through because we know that if there are any mistakes, it's going to be in the copy and not in the reading."

The ability to read music and the technical mastery of your instrument are minimum requirements for a performing career. To develop your skills, take full advantage of all the opportunities your school and community have to offer. Participate in marching, concert and dance bands, jazz and classical ensembles, orchestras, school and church choirs.

Start a vocal or instrumental group of your own and donate (or sell) your services for club meetings, organization dinners, P.T.A. meetings, church picnics, school dances, private parties—any local functions where entertainment would be welcome. The organizational and performing experience will be invaluable.

Get a college degree if at all possible. The music theory and instrumental techniques you can learn at the college level will give you a solid foundation on which to build a performing repertoire.

Above all, practice! Musicians, like athletes, can only keep their "working" muscles in shape through constant exercise. To be a success as a performing musician, you must be at the top of your form at all times. Only frequent practice sessions can keep you in shape.

As basic and essential as technical skills are for a musician or entertainer, it's individual style that makes a performer stand out from the crowd. A singer, for example, is judged on voice and training, but never those qualities alone. Intensity, sincerity, warmth, stage personality and a special, personal way of bringing life to lyrics are what make audiences sit up and take notice.

The only way for a performer to develop a personal style, according to pianist Roger Williams, "is to learn everyone else's style," to find out what's been done and what hasn't.

Williams also believes that musicians should be familiar with as many different styles of music as possible. Comparing music to food, he says, "You need a well-balanced diet. Try them all."

# Careers in Popular Music

Classical training in form, analysis, theory and composition are important to the popular musician. Harmonic knowledge and familiarity with classical technique will broaden your musical horizon. That's especially true today, when so many popular composers borrow from other musical idioms in search of fresh sound combinations.

You can pick up technical skills in the classroom but personal style can only be developed in front of an audience. You need audience reaction to let you know if you're on the right track. Most cities have a number of small clubs that specialize in certain kinds of music—rock, blues, jazz, folk or country. Find the clubs that play your kind of music and get to know the musicians.

## Get to Know Other Musicians

Henry Mancini says: "One of the best ways for an instrumentalist to crack through is to find the people who do the same thing he does. A trumpet player should know every trumpet player in town if he can, because that's the only way he is going to break in. That's how I was able to start in composing film music and it's a technique others I know have used successfully. I met everyone I could who composed film music and little by little they got to know me and started to recommend me for one thing and another. I would say this is the best way to break in unless someone brings you in from the outside."

Getting to know the musicians and getting accepted by them, is a necessary process. Blues pianist Bob Reidy offers some advice from his early days when he was haunting the blues clubs. "Be there night after night," he says, "with your instrument if possible. Wait for a chance to sit in on a jam session. Find out what places, if any, hold amateur nights. Take advantage of any chance you might have to perform in front of an audience. Play as much as you can and practice the rest of the time. Study and play along with recordings of your favorite artists to learn their techniques. Be prepared to give up everything for music."

Reidy's first break didn't make him a star, but it did happen in the best tradition of old Hollywood musicals. One night while he was in a blues club waiting for the band to go on, the pianist became ill and Reidy was asked to fill in on an emergency basis. By being around all the time, he was around at the right time. By constantly practicing and keeping in top form, he was equal to the opportunity when it arose. He was still a long way from his own band and his first album, but he had gotten the break he needed—as a musician among musicians.

Even after that important initial break, things can be rough. Pay is small and bookings are infrequent and uncertain. You will almost certainly need a secondary job of some kind. If you can find work in music education, do so. You'll have the satisfaction of working in your field and many school situations provide some performance opportunities. Also, consider a professional career in addition to music so that you'll have a strong alternative if things don't work out. Even a job driving a cab or tending bar will do on a temporary basis, as long as it provides adequate financial support and leaves you time for your music.

Until you are able to afford an agent or manager, you'll have to solicit your own bookings. Build a press kit as soon as possible, including personal information, photographs and press clippings. A performance tape might also be helpful.

When you start getting bookings, retain an agent or manager. You'll be spending most of your time improving old material and working on new acts and won't have time for financial, legal and public relations work. You should be familiar with the business aspects of performing, even if you have someone else handle them for you.

Your life as a performer in popular music will require long hours, constant travel and meeting tough competition. But the opportunities for a successful career exist if you are willing to work for them. If you believe strongly enough in yourself and have a mature, realistic awareness of what your possibilities are, you could be one of the lucky ones.

# Careers in Symphony Orchestras

Symphony orchestras are a $135 million industry within the performing and visual arts and they offer many opportunities for professional careers. The number of concerts by professional orchestras has doubled in the last decade from 3,843 to 7,535; annually; audiences total 23 million people per season.

Expanding services and expanding budgets need well-trained administrative personnel. Although positions with top U.S. orchestras are still extremely competitive, more opportunities are available today than 15 years ago. Musicians today can earn a substantial livelihood solely as orchestral players. Openings for conductors have also increased with the growth in the number of orchestras with staff expansions of large orchestras.

### Symphony Musicians

More than 1,400 U.S. orchestras provide a wide range of opportunity for musicians to make a career playing symphonic music—from part-time work with largely volunteer community orchestras to full-time activity in polished professional orchestras.

Major orchestras (budgets of more than $1 million) offer their musicians and principal players full-time employment with weekly minimum salaries. Most big-city orchestras have 40 to 52-week seasons, which may include youth concerts, tours and summer or pops engagements in addition to the regular subscription series.

There are about 2,500 players employed full-time by major orchestras. The remainder of the professional symphony musicians in this country—probably another 5,000 to 7,000—hold positions with smaller organizations (budgets under $1 million). Most of these orchestras do not provide a musician's sole income.

Metropolitan orchestras (budgets of $100,000 to $1 million) employ their musicians on a weekly or per-service basis, or a combination of both. Organizations in this category differ widely in how they hire musicians as well as the number and type of concerts given. Many give a majority of their concerts as chamber orchestras or as small ensembles; as few as 10 performances a year may be given by the full orchestra.

Some of these orchestras may employ a core ensemble or quartet on a full-time basis which is then augmented by musicians hired on a per-service basis to accommodate the larger symphonic repertoire. Or they may retain a full-size orchestra on a limited season contract and divide personnel for various services. Professional chamber orchestras usually fall into this small budget category, but generally have longer seasons and pay higher salaries than full symphony orchestras.

The majority of urban and community orchestras with budgets under $100,000 hire musicians on a per-service basis. Yearly salaries depend upon the number of concerts given. Most musicians in these orchestras hold full-time jobs or augment their salaries with private teaching.

Sometimes these part-time orchestra positions are offered in conjunction with college or school faculty positions. A musician working in a large metropolitan area can derive a major part of his income by playing with several community and chamber orchestras, each having a limited number of performances.

Community orchestras may pay their musicians on a per-service basis, or they may only pay section leaders and the concertmaster, the majority of musicians being volunteers.

## Recommended Preparation

Professional musicians need years of private instrumental study behind them before beginning conservatory level training. While completion of a degree program is not essential, most orchestra musicians today have received their training in the country's conservatories and universities.

It's wise to get as much ensemble experience as possible before entering college. Youth orchestras and summer music camps offer excellent opportunities. Apprenticeship with smaller, semiprofessional orchestras enables you to expand your orchestral repertoire before auditioning for a professional position.

The National Orchestral Assn. has sponsored a program for advanced training of young orchestra musicians since 1930. Ninety instrumentalists participate in this training orchestra which helps their repertoire and ensemble abilities. The seven-month season involves three 2½ hour-long rehearsals weekly; the standard training period is three years. The average player's age is 21 and most members have some conservatory or university training.

The Berkshire Music Center's eight-week summer Fellowship Program at Tanglewood, Mass., offers young instrumentalists intensive instruction in orchestral and chamber music playing and an opportunity to work with well-known musicians. All those chosen to participate in the program receive fellowships to cover full tuition costs.

The Aspen Music School offers young musicians an opportunity to play with a variety of orchestral ensembles during a nine-week session each summer. The Festival Orchestra and the Chamber Symphony consist of young professionals and students whose services are contracted through auditions.

The Aspen Philharmonia, the Repertory Orchestra and the String Ensemble are all formed from the student body. Students may attend classes in music literature and theory and take private instrumental lessons and master classes given by noted performers.

Since 1960 the Colorado Philharmonic, a "training orchestra" under the direction of Walter Charles, has given participating young musicians a chance to expand their orchestral repertoire during an intensive eight-week summer season. The orchestra performs three programs each week and a number of special concerts in small communities throughout the state. Seventy young musicians are chosen by audition to participate each year.

The American Symphony Orchestra League's three-week Eastern Institute of Orchestral Studies held each summer at Orkney Springs, Va., offers an opportunity to gain professional performing experience and broaden orchestral repertoire in the context of an intensive conductor training program.

Many American universities and conservatories are well known for training orchestra musicians, among them: Eastman School of Music, Manhattan School of Music, Conservatory of Music at Oberlin College, Juilliard School of Music, Curtis Institute, New England Conservatory, Indiana University, Yale

University, Cleveland Institute and the College-Conservatory of Music at the University of Cincinnati.

One of the newest of these schools is the Shepherd School of Music (Rice University, Houston) which inaugurated a new curriculum in the fall of 1975 to train musicians for careers with symphony orchestras. The focal point of the five-year Orchestral Studies Program is the Orchestra Laboratory which meets regularly both as a full orchestra and in small coaching groups. Students also receive a grounding in music theory, history and applied studies.

## Conducting

Although competition for conducting positions with major orchestras is fierce, there is a continuing opportunity with smaller orchestras and particularly community orchestras. In addition, the expansion of services provided by major orchestras has opened up a new field of secondary positions.

The chief conductor of an orchestra may lead from 30% to 80% of the subscription concerts and make a number of guest conducting appearances in other cities. If he is the music director he generally holds full responsibility for artistic decisions in addition to his conducting duties.

Conducting staffs of major orchestras may also include any of the following: a resident conductor, a principal guest conductor, associate and assistant conductors whose primary responsibilities are often pops or youth concerts. Some staffs include a conducting assistant scheduled to conduct occasionally.

Conductors of many metropolitan orchestras receive most of their income from their orchestras. They conduct the majority of season concerts, sometimes assisted by an associate conductor. The greatest number of conducting opportunities are with community, college and youth orchestras.

These posts are generally held in conjunction with other full- or part-time positions as college or school music teachers, as musicians with larger symphonies or as private music instructors. In many community symphonies the music director also assumes many managerial duties when the orchestra does not have a professional manager.

## Preparation for a Conducting Career

Since the conductor must be a well-developed musician, the following are essential:

*A conductor should have substantial experience as a performer, particularly with ensembles and orchestras. Many great conductors — Monteux, Koussevitzky, Reiner, Toscanini — were instrumentalists first. Youth, high school and college orchestras offer early playing experience.*

*College or conservatory music study should include both choral and instrumental conducting and orchestration courses, as well as a firm background in music history and performance practices. In college, an aspiring conductor should gain as much experience as possible directing student ensembles — which often feature student compositions, pre-Bach music groups and choral ensembles. A well-developed ear and score-reading ability are important. Keyboard facility, particularly the skill of orchestral reduction, is useful.*

*An aspiring conductor should continually strive to widen his exposure to live and recorded performances of all types of music. He should know not only the symphonic repertoire, but all forms of musical expression.*

*Personality is important to the success of a conductor. Vitality and leadership ability should be coupled with fine musicianship.*

## Gaining Experience

A great deal of conducting experience can be gained by participating in college/conservatory student ensembles, by working with small community orchestras (on a volunteer basis) and with youth orchestras at one of more than 300 summer music camps in the country.

Major orchestras like the Baltimore Symphony have from time to time sponsored conductor competitions modeled after the prestigious European competitions.

As part of the Berkshire Music Center's eight-week Fellowship Program, young conductors have a chance to broaden their conducting experience. Under the guidance of well-known conductors, participants work with the Center's orchestra and smaller ensembles. Young conductors are chosen by audition during the winter preceding each session. All those accepted receive fellowships to cover tuition costs.

## Orchestra Administration

The third professional component of an orchestra is its management. Fund-raising, scheduling, public relations, programs and ticket sales are all among the duties of the manager. The degree to which the manager personally handles these tasks depends upon the size of the organization, but he is ultimately responsible for the smooth functioning of all business aspects of the symphony.

Many major symphonies maintain a full schedule for their musicians and have a proportionally large administrative staff —up to 40 people—to handle the many management aspects. A wide variety of skills are required. Each orchestra has its own organizational style and some staff positions may not exist throughout the country. The following descriptions of positions on major orchestra staffs are offered as examples of the types of administrative careers available.

*The chief administrator* of the orchestra may be called president, executive director, general manager, managing director or manager.

The administrator is responsible to the governing board for all aspects of operations including implementation of board policies, long-range planning, contract and labor negotiations, coordination of fund-raising and ticket sales, and supervision of staff.

Salaries for chief administrators of large orchestras are comparable to those paid business executives in similar positions.

If you would like to manage an orchestra, you must have knowledge of all aspects of orchestra operations—budgeting and finance, personnel relations, marketing and even law. You must combine administrative abilities with a knowledge of symphonic repertoire and an understanding of performance standards.

Above all, you should be totally dedicated to the symphony orchestra field and to your own organization. And, be prepared for long days attending concerts, openings, traveling with your orchestra, conducting contract negotiations, etc.

*The assistant manager*, sometimes called the operations manager or manager, assists with management of orchestra operations. These duties usually include coordination of repertoire and guest artists / conductors as well as overseeing administrative personnel.

Depending on the structure of the staff, the assistant may also be responsible for budgets and fiscal affairs, contracts and tour arrangements, as well as for scheduling youth and summer concerts.

*The director of development* is responsible for planning and executing annual fund drives, preparing grant applications and maintaining records of all contributions. The director serves as liaison between the board and committees involved in fund-raising and may also have charge of developing endowment programs.

A solid knowledge of budgets, finance, marketing techniques, mail and fund-raising psychology is essential for this job.

*The director of public relations* promotes symphony events by writing and distributing news releases to various media announcing concert dates, programs, guest artists as well as by arranging for feature stories on the symphony. The public relations specialist arranges press conferences and media coverage of all special symphony events. Duties may include preparation of advertising copy as well as the editing of the program booklets.

*The business manager / controller / bookkeeper* prepares budgets, financial statements and reports, handles account payments, payroll, deposits, tax reports and other financial matters.

*The director of ticket sales* coordinates box office activities, ticket printing, sales reports and supervises the box office staff.

# Careers in Symphony Orchestras

Some orchestra positions do not fall within the administrative category and are often filled by musicians in addition to their regular duties as performers:

*The librarian* maintains and distributes orchestra scores and parts, arranges for purchase or rental of music and enters bowings and other markings into the parts.

*The personnel manager* hires additional musicians as needed or finds substitutes for those unable to perform, sees that musicians meet requirements of attendance, punctuality, dress, etc., and that management provides adequate facilities for the musicians.

This position requires an individual who is fair-minded, diplomatic and has the respect of both musicians and administration.

*The stage manager* has responsibility for seeing that the stage is properly set up and backstage facilities are ready for both rehearsals and performances.

Large metropolitan orchestras usually have a full-time manager, development director, public relations director, accountant/bookkeeper, ticket manager and secretary. Clerical help may be part-time or volunteer. Smaller metropolitan orchestras often pay only the manager on a full-time basis. Most administrative work with community orchestras is handled by volunteers.

## Gaining Experience

There are several opportunities for you to gain experience in orchestra management in preparation for a career in this field.

Volunteer to work part-time or during the summer with a professional symphony orchestra. Few orchestras in this country can afford to turn down a volunteer.

If you are playing with a small orchestra, volunteer to serve as the group's manager.

Combine your college music studies with business. Bachelor of arts programs in arts administration have been instituted at some colleges including Miami University of Ohio and Eastern Michigan University. Graduate degrees in arts administration are conferred by Yale, UCLA and the University of Wisconsin. Harvard's Summer School Institute in Arts Management also offers a program of intensive study.

Martha E. Freitag
American Symphony Orchestra League

# Careers in the U.S. Armed Forces

The recruiting posters tell you to "Join the Navy and see the world." They *could* say "Join any branch of the United States Armed Forces, see the world *and* be a full-time professional musician."

The Army, Navy, Air Force and Marine Corps each maintain various types of musical organizations and offer career opportunities for both string and wind musicians. In addition, positions are available for both men and women as vocalists, accompanists, arrangers, bandsmen, bandmasters, music directors, music librarians, transcribers, orchestra leaders, pianists, recording technicians, instrument repairmen and instructors.

In any branch of the service, a musician can look forward to an enjoyable career, extensive travel and financial security. Benefits include a pay scale that competes with civilian wages, as well as medical care, commissary and post-exchange privileges and retirement pay.

Even if you should decide not to devote your entire career to the service, the training you will receive will be excellent preparation for a civilian music career.

Requirements and opportunities vary from branch to branch, but a high level of musical skill is essential. In each case, auditions are held prior to enlistment. In the Army, Navy and Air Force, recruits complete basic training, then go to the armed forces music training centers. The enlistment contract for the Marine Corps Band assures you that you will neither undergo Marine Corps boot camp, nor be transferred from the Washington, D.C., area.

A solid working knowledge of basic music is a prerequisite for all branches of the armed forces. Practical experience may be gained in dance band, concert band, instrumental ensembles and vocal groups.

Before acceptance into the Navy, an applicant must demonstrate a working knowledge of major and minor scales and the fundamentals of music notation and terminology. You must be able to sight read first-chair parts of standard band literature considered easy to moderately difficult or the second and third-chair parts of literature ranging from moderately difficult to difficult while properly observing phrasing, dynamics and interpretation.

If accepted, you are sent to the Armed Forces School of Music for a 26-week training course. After serving full-time duty with a unit band aboard ship or on a base, you may return to the Naval Music School for advanced training as a conductor, arranger or instructor.

For detailed information about Naval requirements, contact the Navy Department, Music Branch (PERS-724), Washington, D.C., 20730

Auditions for the 138-piece Marine Corps Band are scheduled on the basis of vacancies in the instrumental sections. If you are interested, send a letter of intent and an audition tape including one or two major solo compositions written for the instrument you wish to play to the Operations Officer, U.S. Marine Band, Marine Barracks, 8th and I Sts., SE, Washington, D.C., 20390. A security clearance will be necessary because of the band's close association with the President and the White House.

If you are accepted, you may be assigned to additional duties on the band's supporting staffs, including the band library, operations or instrument repair sections. All band members are appointed staff sergeants upon joining.

*The U.S. Air Force Occupational Handbook* lists as its requirements courses in singing and ear training, piano tuning, conducting, band arranging, composition, principles of musical interpretation and transposition. The service also needs teachers especially qualified in these areas. For information about Air Force bands, contact the nearest Air Force recruiter.

The Army is the largest branch of the armed forces and offers the most opportunities. Most bases in the U.S. and overseas have their own bands, ranging in size from 42 to 100 pieces. The assignment of your choice is guaranteed in writing before enlistment.

Because the Army offers band training in a number of locations, contact your local recruiter for information. He can arrange an audition for you, answer specific questions, and explain in detail the special accelerated promotion opportunities available to all bandsmen under the "Stripes for Skills" program.

If you have a high school diploma and are especially interested in playing in a band, the military services might be just what you're looking for.

To qualify you should know basic music theory and be as skilled on your instrument as possible. Take advantage of all the musical opportunities offered by your school and community. Those best prepared have the greatest chance for acceptance and advancement.

SSgt. Frank Byrnes
U.S. Marine Corps Band

Maj. Marvin E. Keefer
U.S. Army Bands

# Careers in Composing and Arranging

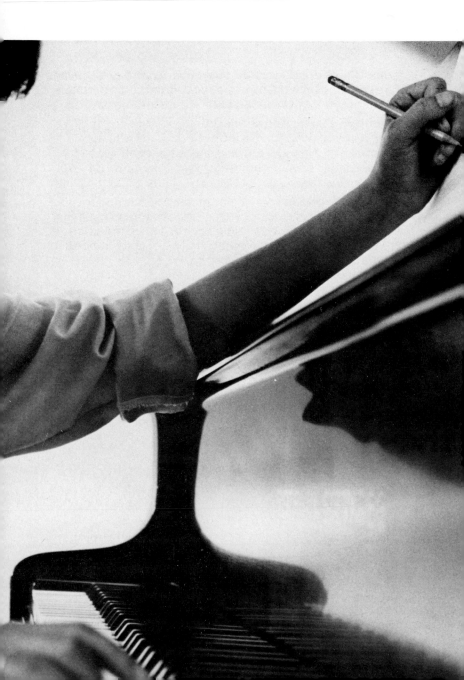

In terms of both dollars and dignity, American composers and lyricists are enjoying unprecedented success. This is particularly true for those who write popular music.

Performing rights organizations report that they collect millions of dollars annually for their composer and lyricist members. Add to these royalties the income that a writer earns from record sales (a penny per "single" by the U.S. Copyright Act of 1901) and sheet music, and you can see that the pot at the end of the rainbow can be a very large one.

However, only a small percentage of those who write popular music ever become successful. Talent and hard work and commitment—years of commitment—often require a healthy dash of luck to bring a writer to the point where he or she can make a living. Many of the successful popular composers today are also performing artists, and their concert tours and personal appearances are major factors in promoting the sale of their records. It seems clear that a bestselling record is the key to a career as a popular composer and especially to the career of a composer who is primarily a songwriter.

This was not always the case. Most of the great songs of the 1920-1950 era were written by people who were either composers and/or lyricists. In recent years a number of young writers decided to become performers to help promote their songs. There is still plenty of room for the nonperforming writer, but it is often easier to make that breakthrough record yourself.

Many of today's songwriters have had musical training in high school, college or with private teachers. Only a few like Henry Mancini and Marvin Hamlisch actually went to conservatories and some of the younger writers were taught to play the piano or guitar by a friend.

Even the hardest of the hard rock creators agree that a writer should learn the techniques that are essential to his or her craft. Mere passion is rarely adequate. It is common for young writers to begin as performers with small groups or to work in local musical theater productions. The more experience that a writer gets in seeing what works musically and how it works, the more quickly the writer will progress. Individuality is still recognized as important and there is limited interest in "another Dylan" or "another Stevie Wonder" or "another Carly Simon." Be yourself and make the best of your own gifts.

One problem that you will face is how to pay the rent and buy the groceries while you are perfecting your craft, while you're making mistakes and learning from them. Many songwriters survive as performers, others as arrangers or teachers. John Denver began as a singing guitar player who joined a folk group, and Burt Bacharach played in nightclubs and accompanied stars in their nightclub performances.

It is extremely unlikely that any young songwriter will achieve success with a first song, and very rare for a composer or lyricist to be able to support himself/herself solely by writing during the first few years. When a writer does make it and his/her works achieve success, those songs can go on earning an income—here and abroad—for many years.

If a song becomes a "standard," it lives on and is performed long after its initial major success. ASCAP records show that a number of composers and lyricists who have not written a best-seller in 20 years are still receiving substantial income from their earlier "standards." Obviously, the creators of today's superhits are earning a lot more, but no one can live on the earnings of just one or two popular songs.

A song may take 10 minutes or 10 months to write, but it usually lasts only a few minutes on a record. It's true that writing music or lyrics—whether popular or serious—requires artistry, but the people who run the record companies and the music publishing firms are businessmen. They appreciate art and talent, but their decisions are made on the basis of commercial reality. It would be naive to look down on these executives. Not only are they very able, but they play a vital role in the music community.

## Getting a 'Hearing'

Beginning songwriters often find it very difficult to get a hearing from record or publishing executives, and many firms won't even open a package that contains an unsolicited manuscript. Don't be discouraged. Try to find someone who knows somebody at one of these companies, and use this personal connection to get a simple tape of your creation to a person in authority. If a publisher likes your song, he can usually get it to a record company executive.

The market for fresh and imaginative music is large and growing daily. The enormous television and motion picture industries are continually searching for talented contemporary composers who can write and arrange well, fast and to order. The musical stage is wide open. Many of today's theater composers started with scores written for off-Broadway nightclub revues or for campus shows.

There are pitfalls and rogues. Just as there are vanity book publishers who will publish your book if you pay for it, there are vanity record companies that suggest glowing possibilities of success if *you* will pay for the cost of making the record. All the U.S. performing rights organizations advise their members to *avoid* any such deals, since it is almost unheard of for any successful record to emerge. In 999 times out of 1,000, only the vanity firm profits.

A number of successful songwriters have polished their skills by working in music publishing firms arranging the works of others. Several major songwriters (including Carole King) have perfected their craft working under contract to large publishing firms.

It is very easy for a young person considering a songwriting career to be discouraged. The odds are that most of those who yearn for such careers and the fame that goes with them will be disappointed. Only a few will ever get any songs commercially published or recorded and an even smaller number of writers will achieve success. But, this tantalizing chance is what inspires the dedicated. A careful, hard-working, talented and committed writer can achieve success while in his or her 20s. There is no single formula or style that is the recommended way to write or learn to write a popular song. The field is wide open even if it doesn't seem to be.

In pursuing your chance, it is important that you protect yourself and your work by copyrighting it before you offer it to a publisher or recording company. The great majority of men and women in the music business are honest people who respect the talents of others, but there are a few who might attempt to appropriate your work. You may secure copyright forms from the U.S. Copyright Office in the Library of Congress, Washington, D.C. Copyrighting is not a complicated process and the fee is not large.

## Writing Symphonic Music

In the symphonic or "serious" music field, the economic picture is somewhat different than in popular music. The financial rewards are much smaller, and the number of American symphonic composers who can support themselves entirely on earnings from their writing is very limited. There are perhaps fewer than 20 composers who do so today.

This may seem shocking until you consider that it costs a great deal to produce a symphonic record, that many fewer symphonic recordings are sold and that these get much less air play on radio and television stations.

Almost every symphony orchestra—large and small—is operating at a deficit and requires subsidies from government or private patrons. The musical director of the Johnny Carson show earns twice as much as the conductor of the New York Philharmonic, and Stevie Wonder or Burt Bacharach will receive more than ten times as much income as such internationally famous composers as Aaron Copland, Samuel Barber or Gian-Carlo Menotti.

There are two major sources of income for young composers in the symphonic field. Many take advanced training in music and music education and with graduate degrees secure jobs on the staff of a high school or college. Teaching provides security for the great majority of serious American composers and this income is often supplemented with grants from foundations or government arts organizations. Composers who have achieved some reputation may also receive additional revenues from commissions to write new works.

A number of universities have composers-in-residence posts which require the composer to do little or no teaching.

There are several other forms of music composition that offer interesting opportunities: Vincent Persichetti of the Juilliard faculty is known for his symphonic works, but he is also widely respected and well compensated for his many excellent pieces for school bands. There is a substantial demand for good choral music for church choirs of all faiths and denominations, and there are positions at music publishing firms for men and women who can produce arrangements of such works.

The great problem for the symphonic composer is to get someone to listen to and play new works. Orchestras devote most of their performances to works written from 50 to 100 years ago. Some composers support themselves as musicians in or con-ductors of symphony orchestras, and these orchestras sometimes play their works. A symphonic composer has to be even more patient and stubborn than someone in the popular field.

A few popular writers may achieve national reputations by the age of 25, but almost no symphonic composer is known nationally before the age of 40. Today, government grants, commissions and the support of the academic community have combined to provide greater economic opportunities for composers than in the past.

If you choose to write operas, symphonies, ballet music or liturgical works you will need to learn specific skills, including how to write a manuscript so that a conductor or performer can play precisely what you had in mind. You must know the limitations and strong points of each instrument and obviously you should be very familiar with the major works in your field.

Acquiring degrees to qualify you for teaching in a music school or conservatory is highly recommended. The pleasant environment of a campus not only provides you with an adequate livelihood, but you usually have time to study, do research and compose. You also have at your disposal competent student instrumental and vocal groups eager to perform worthy new compositions.

The United States is now in the midst of a highly creative musical era. You should approach this opportunity and challenge realistically without losing sight of the importance of personal inspiration. Career planning requires a practical approach, but a career as a composer also requires that magical talent so hard to define.

Walter Wager
American Society of Composers,
Authors and Publishers

# EDUCATION

The music teacher in our school who is helping your youngster to try out a band instrument is:

Robert Klotman, chairman,
music education department,
Indiana University, and president,
Music Educators National Conference

David Whitwell, College Band
Directors National Assn.

Gladys Wright, Women Band
Directors National Assn.

# Careers in Music Education

# Careers in Music Education

Music education begins with the preschool child, carries well beyond the classroom and extends throughout a lifetime to become a prime influence on the musical vitality of the community and the nation. Consequently, a music education career provides an opportunity not only to be involved in the performance of music but to contribute to the process and pleasure of bringing music to others. It is a challenging profession, offering a large measure of personal stimulation and gratification.

## Teaching Qualifications

In its final report, the Music Educators National Conference-Teacher Education Commission recommended the following qualifications for all music educators:

*Personal qualities:* Like all teachers, music educators need first and foremost to be growing human beings.

*They must inspire others:* Continue to learn in their own and other fields; relate to individuals, society and other disciplines and arts; identify and evaluate new ideas; use their imaginations, and understand the role of a teacher.

*Performance abilities:* Music teachers must be able to interpret representative works of the past and present on an instrument or with their voices. They must be able to improvise as well as perform by reading music, playing accompaniments and singing. They should have a basic understanding of the human voice as an instrument and be able to use their own voices effectively. They should be able to conduct as well as supervise and evaluate the performance of others.

*Composition abilities:* Music teachers should be able to organize sounds for personal expression and demonstrate an understanding of the elements of music through original composition and improvisation in a variety of styles. They should be able to identify and explain compositional choices and to notate and arrange sounds for school performances.

*Analytical abilities:* Music teachers should be able to identify and explain compositional devices as they are used in all music, to discuss the results of compositional devices and to describe the means by which the sounds used in music are created.

Since the ability to communicate with students is essential for teachers, music educators must be able to express their philosophy of music and education. They should demonstrate a familiarity with contemporary educational thought and be able to apply a broad knowledge of musical repertoire to the learning problems of music students.

They must be flexible and open-minded to experiments and expanding concepts. New instruments such as synthesizers and other electronic devices have expanded the musical "palette" creating a need for teachers to understand not only the acoustical properties of these instruments but their use in performance.

The term music education covers a spectrum of specialized activities, different for each school organization. However, there are certain common, basic elements which may help you make a career choice.

## Elementary School

Teaching in elementary schools presents by far the greatest opportunity for service in a full or part-time music position. Elementary school music teachers often are expected to integrate music with other subject areas. There are many approaches provided by educators like Kodaly, Orff, Dalcroze and Suzuki that have expanded music learning experiences for children and enriched the total curriculum.

In some communities there is a music specialist for each school responsible for almost all of the musical activities. In other cases, the elementary music teacher, either vocal or instrumental, may visit several schools. In some systems the children come to a music room, while in others the teacher will go to individual classrooms.

In some large school systems, the instrumental teacher may function as a specialist for instruction on strings, woodwinds, etc. However, even these specialists are called upon to combine instruction in overlapping areas: a string teacher may do some wind or percussion instruction or vice versa. In addition to providing instruction to beginners on the various instruments, elementary instrumental teachers also conduct ensembles and are responsible for promoting and developing instrumental programs.

# Careers in Music Education

In many elementary schools, class piano also is offered. Often the teacher is a piano specialist but the assignment may be handled by a competent general music teacher or instrumental instructor.

## The Music Specialist

In many school systems elementary music is taught by the classroom teacher under the guidance of a music specialist. Where this occurs, the specialist plans and guides music learning experiences and assists the classroom teacher. This may include demonstration lessons and regularly scheduled teaching in the elementary classroom. In some school systems the specialist serves as a resource person locating music materials and coordinating music activities that are integrated with school programs and academic areas.

As an elementary music teacher you should be able to play the piano and guitar. You should possess a skilled ear that will perceive pitch and interval variances so that children can develop a degree of pitch discernment, as well as find their singing voices. Furthermore, you need to develop a singing voice that will be an example for children to emulate.

When you assume the role of "specialist" or "coordinator" you also need administrative skills, since you will be part of the administrative staff. Especially important is the ability to work with people.

## Middle or Junior High School

In many smaller school systems the music teacher has a joint junior-senior high or elementary-junior high appointment, and may include a combination of vocal and instrumental music instruction. Larger systems usually have both vocal and instrumental teachers for each school.

The vocal music teacher in a middle or junior high school is normally responsible for the general music class with emphasis on exposure to music rather than performance. Teachers must be prepared to deal with jazz and rock as well as traditional music. They must be sufficiently flexible to devise imaginative projects that will appeal to teenagers and involve them in a variety of musical experiences.

Too many young people have become "musical dropouts" because teachers have lacked imagination to make the program meaningful.

## Senior High School

In smaller communities the high school music teacher may also work in the junior high or the elementary school. However, where there is sufficiently large enrollment in the senior high school, the music teacher usually functions in a single school as a resident vocal or instrumental teacher. Occasionally, where the school population is too small to support a single teacher in both areas or where it may be so large that it requires three or four teachers, the assignments may overlap. An instrumentalist might teach a general music class or one vocal class; a vocalist with an instrumental proficiency might handle a single instrumental section.

In large high schools, with several music staff members, teachers are usually band, orchestra or choral directors. Such schools may expect some prior, successful teaching experience from applicants.

Senior high school music electives include theory, music history and literature, general music, voice classes and small ensembles. Staff members are assigned to these courses according to their training and experience.

The vocal specialist in most secondary schools should have had voice training and some choral conducting. An ability to play piano is required for accompaniments when coaching voices or when an accompanist is not available for rehearsals. Many high schools have a mixed choir, boys' chorus and girls' chorus, all of which may come under the direction of the choral music teacher.

## Instrumental Music

Since no band or orchestra director can rely on students automatically joining the band or orchestra, instrumental teachers must be able to recruit and instruct beginning talent. They may also teach in lower grades to help encourage a continuous supply of instrumental students. It is not unusual to find orchestra and band directors teaching beginning classes in elementary or junior high schools.

In most situations the instrumental teacher must be equipped to teach both wind and string instruments, although some school systems may have wind specialists, string specialists or percussion specialists. Most schools offer both orchestra and band programs and it is incumbent on instrumental teachers to be able to train and conduct such ensembles.

Instrumental instructors today should also be prepared to teach jazz programs which are becoming more and more a part of the regular school curriculum.

## Administering School Music Programs

Many communities have a supervisor of music or a director of music education. In a large system the director or head of music education may have a staff of music supervisors with specific assignments for different grade levels. Administrators are responsible to the superintendent and his staff.

Individuals in this aspect of music education usually have had a number of years of successful teaching and training well beyond the master's degree. Among the responsibilities are budget planning, staffing, providing facilities, public relations, in-service workshops, examining and selecting equipment and textbooks, preparing reports and other areas that lead toward improved school instruction.

Music supervisors are regarded as the community's administrative leaders in music education. They represent the music department at school administration meetings including meetings of the board of education, and generally speak for the music department before the public.

They often are members of civic and symphony boards, may be members of professional music organizations and participate in their activities.

In large communities where there is a hierarchy of staffing, the supervision of classroom instruction is a responsibility of the supervisors. These individuals spend most of their time in the schools working with students and teachers. They demonstrate teaching techniques, provide in-service training courses for classroom teachers, evaluate instruction and coordinate large district or city programs.

A supervisor or director of music should enjoy working with people, both adults and children, and have a personality that instills confidence and elicits cooperation from the staff. He/she also should possess musical ability that commands the respect of the community's musicians. With these qualities, a supervisor will enhance the overall position of music in the school system.

## State Supervisors of Music

The number of state supervisors of music has increased and with this increase in number their role as state representatives for music education has taken on added significance. They serve as resource and staff personnel to state departments of education which, in turn, make recommendations to state legislatures.

State supervisors of music also serve as liaison between disciplines. They help to coordinate and integrate music with other subject areas in curricular matters. They also assume leadership in setting standards for classroom instruction as well as help to enforce standards for certification of teachers.

In selecting state supervisors of music, committees usually seek individuals with years of successful teaching experience in a variety of situations, preferably at all grade levels and in both vocal and instrumental music. Because these positions are dependent upon funds allocated by state legislatures, state supervisors do not always receive a salary commensurate with their experience and the responsibilities of the position.

Just as in any administrative position, state supervisors must possess skills in working with people , be convincing in their knowledge of their subject area, and capable of inspiring both laymen and music teachers in order to strengthen the role of music as an integral part of education. They should be skilled as musicians as well as teachers. They ought to have a broad cultural background and be able to see music not as a separate, isolated subject but as one that is part of the total educational matrix.

The state supervisor of music keeps his state's music teachers abreast of current developments in music education, is available for consultation and gives advice to expand music programs as well as improve instruction.

## Training for Music Education

In the United States, there is no central agency for the licensing of teachers. Each state sets its own requirements and issues the necessary licenses to teach within its boundaries. However, there is general agreement among states on qualifications and a great deal of reciprocity. You should check with the appropriate state department of education for information on licensing or certification requirements. The music education department at any college or university may also be able to assist you in determining certification requirements for a specific state.

The MENC Commission on Teacher Education recommends that the prospective music educator have the following background:

*Precollege preparation in musical performance on piano as well as experience with instrumental and vocal ensembles; a knowledge of basic musicianship; some music history and repertoire; conducting, leadership and teaching experiences.*

*A general college education including courses in humanities, natural sciences, mathematics and social studies.*

*Basic musicianship and performance involving listening, improvisation, composition, aural analysis, history and criticism. Instruction should be designed to integrate the study of music theory, history and performance in the development of comprehensive musicianship.*

*Studies should emphasize functional knowledge of the language and grammar of music; the ability to hear and grasp the basic elements of musical compositions; an understanding of the methods by which music is conceived, constructed and scored.*

*Performance skills should include conducting, score reading and rehearsal techniques as well as sufficient proficiency on piano, guitar or another appropriate instrument to be able to demonstrate musical concepts or accompany the class.*

*You should have a major performance area in which you can give an accurate and musically expressive performance, and have the ability to improvise inventively.*

*It's wise to have a minor performance area in which you develop the ability to play representative band and orchestra instruments and to use your voice in demonstrations.*

*You should have ensemble performance experience in large and small groups.*

*The prospective music educator should also have a good professional background in teaching. Studies should include demonstration, observation and other laboratory experiences along with student teaching; practical application of the principles of educational psychology to music teaching, and the philosophical and social foundations of music education.*

*Above all, to succeed as a music educator, you must be enthusiastic, intellectually alive and a sensitive human being. You must exhibit personal qualities of leadership, intellectual curiosity, social commitment and a basic knowledge of your role as a teacher.*

## Interviewing for a Position

When applying for a position, the initial contact is probably the most difficult one. First, you must determine your area of interest and establish a priority list in your mind. For example, if you wish to teach in a high school, then you must recognize that many high schools require prior experience. If you like a particular school system, you should be prepared to accept a junior high or middle school assignment to gain the necessary experience and progress through the system.

If you are a vocal major who wishes to conduct choirs, you should keep in mind that there are few such exclusive assignments. Most vocal teachers work in other related areas such as general music, voice classes, theory, etc. Instrumental assignments in high schools often involve a combination of theory, music appreciation and other subjects. It is important to remember that the perfect job probably does not exist. When applying for a position, you must be prepared to assume obligations that may not always be at the top of your priority list.

During the interview you should bear in mind that most interviewers are interested in how you think and how musical you are. You should be prepared to perform in some manner to demonstrate "musicality". For musicians, this is an accepted procedure. Usually the focus of the interview or audition is based on the vacancy that is being filled. For example, if an elementary job is open, you might be asked to play a simple song accompaniment on the piano or guitar. If applying for a high school orchestra position, you may be asked to perform on your major instrument and / or conduct a page from a score.

It is not improper to inquire beforehand about the nature of the audition-interview if one is required. Interviews are a means of gaining experience as well as finding out all the appropriate information about a vacancy.

## Finding a Job

Any capable individual willing to work in a geographic area that has a serious shortage of teachers, such as inner-cities or rural communities, will probably find a job. If you are seeking employment in areas where there are special problems you must not only be knowledgeable in your subject but be sufficiently secure to be able to cope with unusual situations. You should have some background in sociology and psychology. It is especially desirable that you do your student teaching where similar conditions prevail.

If you are seeking a job in a particular part of the country, you should apply through the personnel offices of surrounding communities as well as in the specific location you seek. Nearly all universities have placement bureaus that assist in placing graduates. These agencies are effective but you should not rely entirely on them.


Dr. Robert Klotman
Indiana University
President,
Music Educators National Conference

# Careers in Band Directing

# Careers in Band Directing

A career as a college band director means first and foremost being a serious conductor. The band director shares the basic goals and techniques with even the most famous of orchestral conductors.

The primary difference between the two is choice of literature. As a band director you'll have an opportunity to perform and actively participate in contemporary music. You'll work primarily with literature written for the wind ensemble (or band medium) rather than for the orchestra.

You'll also have a special responsibility to educate your students. You'll provide your students with a sampling of the best original wind music of the past three centuries in a well-planned program spanning perhaps two or three years.

It will be your job to provide the unique form of education which comes only through the live performance of music and exposure to the intuitive and aesthetic nature of music. You'll also present pertinent background and biographical material and technical discussions regarding the music which is being performed.

It should be noted that the responsibilities and training for a high school band director are similar to that of his or her college counterpart. (Indeed, most college band directors get their start at the high school level.) However, because the high school band director works with young and often inexperienced students, he or she spends more time teaching instrumental techniques.

The band director, like all conductors, must also have administrative skills. Among the details you'll be responsible for are scheduling and presenting concerts and concert tours, recruiting and training new musicians for ensembles, and a variety of advertising and clerical tasks vital to the operation of any concert organization.

While the most important part of the band director's job is the role of serious conductor, almost every band director has important nonconcert obligations. Most typical of these is the preparation of shows for football season. At larger universities, this is often a separate, specialized position. In any case, the band director with this responsibility must design, rehearse and present a complete entertainment package—usually a different one for each game.

As a band director, you'll choose and sometimes arrange music, teach the rudiments of marching, design the visual aspects of the band's performance, choose props and write the script. You may contribute student musicians to other sports on campus (such as basketball); however, these are usually smaller pep bands, often organized and run by the students themselves.

What sort of training is needed to prepare you for such a broad range of responsibilities?

You should, first of all, plan to be a music major when you enter college, and if possible select your college on the basis of its band program. Much of the training is acquired on the spot as you observe the college band director at work and see how your college band functions. To attend a college which doesn't have a strong and well-rounded band program would place you at a serious disadvantage.

Almost every state requires a teaching certificate before you can be employed as a high school band director. So it's advisable that you concentrate on the field of music education. However, this almost necessary choice of curriculum doesn't adequately provide the depth of musical training needed for dealing with important music literature, since the courses required for certification in many states are not those which are crucial to the musical development of a serious conductor.

In a 1974 survey of more than a thousand high school band directors, the College Band Directors National Association (CBDNA) found that 88% of the directors wished they had had more ear training; 87% wished they had had more conducting experience and sight singing; 85%, more theory; 79%, more keyboard; 78%, more music history, and more than 50% wished they had had more training in musical styles.

These areas are fundamental to the basic musical training for conducting.

It's impossible to concentrate on all of these areas while meeting the education requirements of the various state certification boards. You might therefore consider other ways to obtain this essential part of your education, such as pursuing advanced degrees in theory and history, rather than in music education.

# Careers in Band Directing

In any case, a band director must be self-motivated for a lifetime of study and improvement of basic musical skills.

In addition to cultivating basic music skills, you'll need certain technical expertise to prepare you for this profession. The first of these is the development of proficiency on at least one wind instrument. By reaching a highly skilled level of performance you'll gain technical insights necessary for conducting. But, more important, as Bruno Walter once said, "No one should even think of studying to be a conductor until he has exhausted the expressive abilities of his own instrument."

Other skills necessary for being a band director relate to the requirement of the position itself. The CBDNA survey found that most successful high school band directors thought they were not adequately prepared in these skills during their own college training. The survey revealed that 89% of those responding indicated they should have had more training in brass and woodwind classes; 86% indicated they would have liked more training in percussion; 85% in instrumental methods and literature; 82% in marching band; 76% in band arranging; 66% in band administration, and 64% in instrument repair.

While no college will ever be able to provide all that is necessary in a four-year undergraduate curriculum, you shouldn't be alarmed because many of these skills can be learned on the job and from one's colleagues.

Several journals, read regularly by almost all successful band directors, devote extensive coverage to these areas; there are also numerous conventions, such as that of the CBDNA, which enable you to share first-hand in the knowledge and experience of your colleagues throughout the country.

After you've had your initial training, how do you go about becoming a band director? Most band directors begin their careers in the public schools. Information regarding openings and vacancies can be obtained from your state education office.

Placement offices at all major universities carry listings of openings at both the college and high school levels. Your own college band director can be a valuable source of information. If he belongs to the CBDNA, he has opportunities to learn of professional positions throughout the country.

Once you've acquired a position as a band director and begin to accumulate experience, advancement is often a very simple process—even automatic—for those with ability. Almost every successful high school band director periodically receives offers to move to a larger school system or to the college level.

Opportunities for advancement for you as a band director will come much faster and more often than for your colleague who teaches music only in the classroom. Why? Because of the band director's high degree of public exposure.

While the subject of accountability is a very complex one for the classroom teacher, the band director and his work are always out in the open where they are subject to either criticism or praise. So, if you're competent, there are usually very few obstacles to advancement which can be placed before you.

If you begin in the public schools, you can generally expect to advance as far as your talent and education permit. It is generally agreed that the highest level that one can expect to achieve in this profession is a position as band director at a "Big Ten" school, as well as at a handful of prestigious universities such as UCLA.

Band directors who advance to major universities have many additional fringe benefits such as opportunities for guest conducting. Most college band directors view guest conducting as one of the most exciting and valuable activities. It brings added exposure, travel opportunities and, of course, additional financial rewards—often amounting to several hundred dollars a day plus expenses.

Being a successful band director, however, requires a substantial investment of your time, energy and personal involvement. It's difficult to "turn off" when you go home at the end of the day.

But for the most successful band directors, the positive aspects—travel, public exposure and financial rewards—compensate for the time and energy required.

Finally, and perhaps most significantly, a career in the field of music rarely seems like "work."

In fact, a well-known college band director recently commented: "I have been in this business for 25 years and feel like I've never worked a day."

While every occupation has its moments of routine and frustration, it's difficult to think of a career that has greater personal rewards than that of being a musician, especially a conductor.

If you'd like further information on career opportunities in this area, talk to your own high school band director. He can be a valuable source of information and a dependable counselor as well.

## Opportunities for Women

According to a recent survey by the Music Educators National Conference (MENC), women hold a whopping 80% of all general music teaching jobs and 17% of all public school instrumental posts.

Of the 50,000 band directors in this country roughly, 6% (3,000) are women. Women instrumentalists are found primarily on the elementary and junior high level (65%) or the high school level (33%). Only 2% teach in colleges and universities.

You'll find, however, a growing number of professional opportunities in band instruction becoming available to women. The large number of men band directors is a reflection of the band's military history and the western world's historical exclusion of women from some performing arts.

Today, women are marching in nearly every university band in the nation. Result: more jobs open to women in school band instruction. At the amateur level, women represent 14% of all percussionists and 20% of all brass players.

As a band director, you can find teaching opportunities at most levels although a majority of women currently directing are with elementary bands (grades 4-6), junior high school bands (grades 7-9) and with combination kindergarten-through-eighth grade groups in smaller schools.

About 40% of women band directors teach at the elementary level. To teach at this level, you'll need an interest in, and rapport with, young children as well as lots of patience.

These positions require limited amounts of "outside" time, usually for recruitment, school assemblies and during the Christmas season for special programs.

Junior high schools currently provide jobs for about 30% of women directors. At this level, you'll teach music fundamentals rather than become involved in extensive marching experience. Often you are free to build your own band program within the community structure. However, be prepared to have your school serve as a feeder to the high school band and thus have your program influenced by that of the high school band director.

Should you want to teach at the high school level—where 5% of women band directors currently work— you'll find increased salaries along with more responsibilities and added demands on your time.

You can expect to devote more of your free time to band instruction—possibly two nights a week and half of the Saturdays during the school year.

Be practical when selecting a university or college. Choose one which has a reputation for giving women equal opportunities. Consider the number of women band members, the amount and quality of assistance you'll receive in future job placements, and the philosophy of the school's band directors and other instrumental instructors.

After you've enrolled in the school of your choice, become active and volunteer for work in the band department. The skills you'll pick up in working on uniforms or in the music library will be helpful later in your own career. Attend state music meetings, participate in music camps and summer sessions, take advantage of opportunities to travel with music groups.

Summer vacations and holidays are an excellent time to return to your high school and offer to help the school band director with performance preparations—especially for football season or just before a competition.

By giving a little extra and taking advantage of every musical possibility, you'll not only broaden the scope of your own education, but will acquire additional skills that will serve you in your career.

Whether your extra activities result in a job or not, however, every musical experience you have will benefit you in some way. But volunteer work is only one direction. Other good resources are professional meetings, participation in music organizations, music festivals, contests and clinics.

In preparing for a career as a band director, you'll also want to consider the problems of combining your work with marriage.

Marriage and a career can be compatible. It is easier if your husband is in a similar or complementary career. Or, you can limit your work to the elementary or junior high level where demands are considerably fewer than on the high school or college level.

Your organizational abilities will come in handy in managing your work load as well as a home and family.

Remember that once you've "settled" into your first professional job, it's not *where* you are that's important but *what* you do when you get there.


David Whitwell
College Band Directors National  Assn.

Gladys Wright
Women Band Directors National Assn.

# Careers in Private Teaching

# Careers in Private Teaching

If you are interested in teaching music, you should be aware that working in a school situation is not your only career possibility. Give some thought to going into business for yourself. Good, well-qualified private music teachers are always in demand. As a private instructor, you will have the satisfaction of sharing your mastery of vocal or instrumental music with others—and of being your own boss while you do it.

Private teaching is very flexible. It can be a full-time career or a part-time means of supplementing your income. You plan your own schedule, so your work week can be as long or as short as you wish. You can work out of your own home or rent a studio in another location, such as a retail music store.

Many music stores have instrumental instruction programs that utilize private teachers. In some cases the teachers are salaried employees, either full or part-time, who also serve on the sales staff or as teaching program coordinators. In other instances, teachers may rent studio space from the store and collect fees for themselves from the students. Some use in-store space free of charge.

You will find that the opportunities for a full-time career as a private teacher will vary from place to place, and will be best in middle or upper-income neighborhoods and communities, especially those with strong existing band and orchestra programs. No matter how excellent a school music program is, the number of students involved often prevents the director from giving each student the individual attention he or she may need. Private lessons on a one-to-one basis can be an invaluable supplement to school programs. Make a point of checking out the competition in any given area, however. Your specialty may already be taught by several others.

The greatest demand is for teachers of piano, organ and guitar. These are by far the most popular instruments among America's amateur musicians, and are not taught as part of the school music curriculum as often as band instruments.

Parents who want to introduce their children to music often begin with the piano, because piano lessons can be started at an earlier age than the study of most other instruments. Interest in the guitar, especially among teenagers and young adults, is growing rapidly and qualified teachers have little trouble attracting students.

Many private teachers are exploring group instructional methods, which are especially applicable to the teaching of piano and guitar. For some teachers, group instruction is more challenging than one-to-one teaching, and is, of course, more remunerative. Before entering a group teaching situation, be sure to investigate the large number of commercially available programs. You may want to use an existing method or create your own. Group guitar lessons can easily be organized in the home. All you need is a well-lighted space, a blackboard and some folding chairs. Group piano requires more than one instrument and is most convenient in a studio situation.

As a part-time occupation, private teaching can bring added income to anyone skilled enough on an instrument to teach it. If you play well, but intend to go into some other line of work, consider offering lessons evenings and weekends. If you want to stay home and raise a family, you can teach in the home and keep an eye on the children at the same time. As a music student, you can help pay for your education by teaching. As an in-school music teacher, you will find private lessons a profitable way to spend your vacations.

Private teaching is an ideal part-time occupation for performing musicians as well. In addition to the extra money—an important factor in a field where bookings can be irregular—you will find teaching to be a way to refine your own musical skills.

If you are a member of a drum and bugle corps, there may be a place for you as an instructor when you leave the corps. Drum corps often have as many as 15 part-time teachers in such specialized areas as drilling and color guard choreography, as well as trumpet and percussion techniques. The corps will pay a small fee for part-time teachers during the winter practice season, and a larger stipend during the busy summer competition period. Teachers usually travel with the corps during the summer, with all expenses paid.

To succeed as a private music teacher—full or part-time and no matter what instrument you choose—you should be able to play better than your best pupil. If you intend to teach elementary piano or guitar, you can get by on limited skills. You would be better advised, however, to get the best training possible. The more versatile you are, the better your chances for success will be.

Know the capabilities of your instrument and be able to demonstrate them. A degree in music from a college or conservatory is desirable, but extensive performing experience can be substituted. Keep active musically.

In addition to being a fine musician yourself, you must also have an aptitude for teaching. You will need patience and an ability to accomplish musical objectives quickly and successfully. Being able to generate enthusiasm as you teach is also essential. Learning should be fun for your students. If you are going to college, include courses in methods of teaching music in your studies. Join professional music organizations so you can associate with your fellow teachers.

To be a good teacher, you must enjoy teaching and the creative process of turning your students into musicians themselves. Remember that a good teacher always remains a student himself—searching constantly for better ways to improve his teaching and keeping abreast of new developments in his field.

The information in the chapter which follow was compiled with the assistance of:

Elmer Brooks, Aeolian American Corp., for the National Piano Manufacturers Assn.

James H. Burton, Piano Technicians Guild

CBS Musical Instruments [The Steinway Company; Rogers Drums]

C. G. Conn, Ltd.

Leonard Dreyer, Grossman Music, for the National Association of Musical Merchandise Wholesalers

William Gard, National Association of Music Merchants

Theodore M. McCarty, Bigsby Accessories, Inc.

Morton Manus, Alfred Publishing, for the National Music Publishers Assn.

C. F. Martin Organisation

Dr. Robert Moog, Moog Music

Vito Pascucci, Leblanc Corp.

The Selmer Company

# Careers in Music Retailing

# Careers in Retailing

If you play an instrument, chances are it came from one of the 6,000 retail music stores that employ thousands of people in every capacity from manager to teacher to instrument repair specialist.

While there are a few retail chains with stores in several states, most owners operate just one or two stores and get involved in every aspect of their business.

There are three types of music retailers: the full line dealer who carries all types of instruments and accessories (sometimes television sets and recording equipment, too); the dealer specializing in band instruments and amplification equipment, and the keyboard dealer who concentrates on pianos and organs.

Many retailers also have flourishing instructional programs which require studio space and a sizeable teaching staff.

Regardless of the dealer's specialty or the depth of his music service capability, the basic skill required in retailing is sales.

## Sales Opportunities and Professional Qualifications

Anyone with a gift for persuasion and a sense of conviction can sell. But in a music store you'll be in a better position to counsel the customer if you can play an instrument.

Because retailing is growing more complex, an increasing number of managers look for employees with college degrees.

Many colleges now offer a combined music/business degree program for musically oriented individuals who wish to pursue nonperforming careers.

Some colleges with good programs in this subject area are Bradley University, Peoria, Ill.; Indiana University at Evansville; University of Miami, Coral Gables, Fla.; Mount Senario College, Ladysmith, Wisc., and Foothills College, Los Altos Hills, Calif.

Many of the larger music retail stores (usually those in the full line category) cooperate with area colleges and universities in providing internships or work-study programs for students enrolled in joint degree programs.

Smaller retail operations may have entry-level openings for students without college training who have a deep interest and performing proficiency in music.

However, if you're considering music retailing, be realistic about the possibilities of advancement to a management position—especially if you have competition from employees with business administration courses or degrees.

If you can't afford to attend college full-time, you may want to consider enrolling in evening courses in business and retailing to augment your interest in the music field.

Many music retailers seeking college-trained employees rely on the recommendations of music educators from area colleges and universities whose judgment they trust. The top management of large, multistore operations often recruit on college campuses across the country for their beginning management and sales personnel. But the noncollege trained person with an interest in music can usually explore job opportunities by establishing personal contact with local music retailers.

Where you want to work—and live—obviously depends on your lifestyle and career values. But you should be realistic about the possibilities: there are more guitar players who want to live and work in San Francisco than North Dakota. But your chances of getting an entry-level position in a music store in North Dakota are far greater than they would be in San Francisco.

## What's In It For Me?

Annual salaries for salesmen in a retail store vary, depending upon ability, motivation and the reputation of the store for which they work. Store location, the brands of instruments the store carries and the promotion, advertising and public relations undertaken by the store owner and his manufacturer considerably influence the earnings of the sales staff.

If you are a salesman who travels on behalf of your employer in a given area, you will obviously be less affected by the location of your employer's store but will, nevertheless, be dependent upon the store's reputation for delivery and service as well as the quality of its product lines.

Whether you work in a store or travel for your employer, you may be paid in a variety of ways. Some salespeople work on a straight commission, particularly "supersalesmen" who feel they can earn more in this way. Most salespersons, however, are more comfortable with the security of a combined salary-and-commission, that is, a monthly base salary with commission over a given number of sales.

## Where Do I Fit In?

Depending upon the type of music store in which you work, you may sell pianos, wind instruments or even accessories. Chances are you'll find yourself under the wing of an experienced salesman or sales manager who will work with you.

As in any other business situation, you'll be on trial with the store management for a specified period of time; you'll also undoubtedly be on a rotating sales assignment, depending upon the number of departments in your store.

You'll fit in with the store management and other salespeople if you share their interest in music and their conviction that they are selling a valued commodity—music and its enjoyment—to their customers.

The National Association of Music Merchants (NAMM) has a series of cassette tapes entitled "The Business of Music" covering a variety of selling approaches and problems.

If you want a head start on your selling career while still a student, check with the music department or library since many colleges offering joint business/music degrees have these tapes in their student libraries.

## Teaching Opportunities in Music Stores

Many large stores have extensive studio operations, often managed by an educational director. In many instances the educational director is also the store's contact with music teachers in private studios, public and parochial elementary and secondary schools, area colleges and conservatories. He is often regarded by the store staff as an authority in the music-education field.

The in-store educational director usually has at least a bachelor's degree in music education (preferably a master's degree) and has had teaching experience. Such a background makes him the professional equal of teacher-customers and tends to attract these people to his store.

The educational director arranges store recitals, oversees the entire educational operation and often leads workshops for music teachers.

He may also initiate in-school group instruction programs (working with local faculty members); arrange band and orchestra competitions; work with community band programs, and engage in public relations efforts which help promote store sales.

## Becoming a Sales Manager

In a larger, full line store, there are managers for each department. They supervise sales personnel and participate in the general operation of the store. Sales managers usually rise from the ranks of sales personnel after proving their abilities.

Age and seniority are not the only criteria for advancement. Extensive knowledge of a particular product area (such as guitars and amplifiers) can help promote a young person quite quickly to a supervisory post.

Sales managers are also involved in ordering merchandise, evaluating inventory and turnover and setting performance standards and sales quotas for all personnel.

Stores that operate more than one retail outlet usually choose outstanding sales managers to operate the individual outlets. Once again, the criteria for advancement to store manager are administrative and sales ability and a firm grounding in the business skills needed to run a retail store for maximum profit.

## Other Management Opportunities

In medium and large-sized music retail outlets other management opportunities may include being a department or division manager, such as in sheet music, repair and service, shipping or small goods (accessories) departments. These opportunities, as well as that of the sales manager, are prerequisites for becoming the general manager of the entire store.

## Opportunities in Service and Repairs

With increased consumer concern about the reliability of products, service and repair departments are becoming more important.

# Careers in Retailing

The enormous number of new electronic music instruments in recent years has opened up additional career opportunities for repair and service personnel. Technical training in electronics—coupled with visits to and classes at the factories of major electronic instrument manufacturers—are prerequisites for long-term employment in such departments.

Many stores require that each new employee spend a certain amount of time in the service and repair departments to gain first-hand knowledge of the items sold and serviced.

### Starting Your Own Music Store

The person who establishes a retail music store has generally had experience selling musical instruments, accessories and supplies. A store owner should be well-trained in business administration, merchandising, advertising and promotion, sales and personnel management. Most successful music retailers have risen through the ranks and have combined a college degree in business or music with an inherent love of music and practical selling experience.

But one must also have substantial capital backing to start a retail music store since manufacturers will obviously not sell their products to a retailer who cannot afford to pay his bills.

One of the most useful publications about starting a music store is "Starting and Managing a Small Retail Music Store," available from the Superintendent of Documents, U.S. Government Printing Office, Washington, D.C., 20402. If you're considering opening a retail music outlet, it's a good idea to send for this inexpensive government publication.

The major requisites for a successful music store owner are:

1. Sufficient capital backing and a source of financing.
2. A good store location—in the right market.
3. Business acumen, sensitivity to people and a solid educational background in business administration and music.
4. Administrative ability and management skills.

5. Demonstrated salesmanship.

6. Ability to play an instrument and an interest in music and music performance.

7. Interest in the field of music education—knowing the latest trends at all levels of school music instruction as well as the teaching approaches and programs of major manufacturers and manufacturers' associations. This interest and knowledge is necessary to sell convincingly to school administrators, music educators and private and group music teachers.

8. A good personal and professional relationship and rapport with private and group teachers, school music personnel and college music faculty members as well as church and civic music personnel.

9. A strong sense of public and community relations—being truly involved in the community in which the business is located.

The successful music retailer never really stops selling—even when he can afford to hire all the sales personnel he wishes. He remains active in professional associations, educator groups and civic and business organizations at the local, state and national levels.

William Gard
National Association of
Music Merchants

# Careers in Manufacturing

Employment opportunities in manufacturing have grown steadily over the years as increased interest in making music has swelled the ranks of amateurs and the demand for instruments.

While some instruments such as accordions, harmonicas and violins are still produced largely in Europe, American-made pianos, guitars and band instruments are the finest in the world.

The most recent additions to the music manufacturing scene are instruments requiring electronic circuitry such as organs and synthesizers. The first electric organs were developed in the 1930s, but the first synthesizer was not produced commercially until 1964. In fact, American developments in electronics have resulted in a new generation of sound that has widened business horizons, too. Today sound amplification and modification systems are one of the fastest growing areas related to musical instrument manufacturing.

## The Production Staff

For centuries the production of musical instruments was traditionally the work of skilled artisans who carefully hand-crafted and assembled the various pieces. Some of the hand-crafting aspects of manufacturing have been changed by technological advances of the past 50 years. Assembly-line methods, new materials such as plastics, and electronics have greatly affected the industry.

There is still, however, a place for the skilled craftsman. The range of job opportunities, in fact, is greater than ever before because in many cases modern advances have been used to supplement rather than replace traditional methods.

While some basic components of musical instruments can be machine made, trumpets, pianos, guitars, clarinets, violins and drums still require many of the hand skills that have long been associated with the production of quality instruments.

Different skills are required for the manufacture of different instruments. There is a need in all phases, however, for tool and die makers, assemblers, screw machine operators, buffers, sanders and tuners.

# Careers in Manufacturing

Manufacturers of brass and some woodwind instruments have positions for die casters, solderers, engravers, lacquerers, platers, valve makers and others skilled in assembling the various elements as the instrument nears completion.

The newer instruments—organs and synthesizers—require the talents of engineers who understand microcircuitry and computer technology. Since the new electronic instruments contain chips to handle a multiplicity of functions, engineers must understand not only the functions of the components, but their musical potential as well.

Pianos, despite changes in style and appearance, are basically the same instruments they've always been. Modern production methods may be employed for the manufacture of metal interior pieces, and for primary woodworking, veneering and mill operations, but the final product is a result of handcrafting and skilled artisanship.

Likewise, there are few shortcuts in the manufacture of quality guitars, violins or cellos. Highly refined woodworking skills are necessary for the production of a good stringed instrument. In addition, the best guitars and mandolins are usually embellished with decorative carving or inlay.

Among traditional musical instruments, drums have benefited most from the development of new materials. Plastics have replaced hides on the drum heads, and are widely used for the bodies. The finished drum, however, still requires handwork. Skilled craftsmanship is necessary for gluing joints, centering the head, trimming, sanding and tuning.

The final assembly of any instrument, in fact, is reserved for the most highly skilled members of the production staff. A long training period is frequently required.

After completion each instrument is evaluated by a tester before it leaves the plant. Testers must be musicians as well as craftsmen, familiar with the instrument and its musical capabilities, *and* able to make minor adjustments or pinpoint problems for adjustment by others on the production line.

While some of the production functions can be handled by someone without musical training, knowing how to play the instrument is an important asset.

According to one manufacturer, in the music business, knowing how to play an instrument might be compared to having a college degree in another field. In many instances, it will be helpful in progressing to a more skilled, better paying job.

If you are interested in a career in musical instrument manufacturing, you can find job opportunities all over the country, but will have the best luck in the Midwest, which is the center of the band instrument industry. About 50 per cent of all American instrument manufacturers are located in the Midwest, 43 per cent within an hour's drive of Chicago.

The supply industries for the various manufacturing segments—those making cast iron plates, actions, keyboards, hardware, tuning pins, strings, mouthpieces, etc.—are generally located near the site of the instrument being manufactured.

For a career in instrument manufacturing, you must meet age requirements of various states as well as labor and insurance laws. You don't need any basic skills for a beginning job other than the ability to learn, since most manufacturers have on-the-job training programs. Some firms also have apprenticeship programs for the more skilled craft jobs.

Most production workers belong to a labor union, although there are still a few open shops. A workweek consists of five eight-hour days with overtime pay for more than 40 hours of work. This may vary since some companies work longer hours during the production season but may close the plant for a month-long summer vacation.

In most organizations, production management personnel are recruited from the ranks of the experienced and skilled production staff. Management-level personnel can often, however, move to other companies in the industry, or even to management jobs in different fields entirely.

# Careers in Manufacturing

### The Inventors

Another important possibility for a career in instrument manufacturing is the area of design and development. Often specialists in other fields, such as electronics and engineering, or musician/performers, have created new instruments which have led to the development of new industries.

Among the more influential have been John Philip Sousa (the sousaphone); Laurens Hammond (electric organ); Harold Rhodes (electric piano); Dr. Robert Moog and RCA engineers Harry Olson and Herbert Belar (the synthesizer).

Hundreds of others have made refinements in the basic instrument or have created accessory items, amplification equipment and adaptors which have broadened the capabilities of the instruments or made them easier to play.

If you have mechanical talent and an inventive mind, you will find opportunities with manufacturers who seek to expand their product lines or make improvements on existing instruments.

### The Sales Organization

After manufacture, instruments can be sold directly to the retail music stores or handled through jobbers, wholesalers or distributors.

Most manufacturers have a field sales organization consisting of representatives strategically located throughout the country, with responsibility for a particular territory. A few companies use the services of manufacturers' representatives who handle several brand names.

To be a sales representative, you must be knowledgeable about your product and must establish good business relations with retailers in your area. The job requires knowledge of retail sales, advertising, store display, retail personnel relations, credit and collections, and an up-to-the-minute familiarity with the market and competitive conditions. For this (and other) sales jobs, you must be a "self-starter," dependable and able to communicate. You need not be able to play a musical instrument.

Compensation is usually excellent and relates to dollar volume of sales by territory. It is paid in the form of salary plus reimbursed expenses, commission and expenses, or a combination of both.

Sales reps may report to a regional field representative, but most often work directly with the company sales manager, who is located at or near company headquarters. The sales manager, using product and market studies and statistics developed from company and industry experience as well as outside mercantile information, must project instrument requirements for months ahead to be used as a production guide.

Overall, the sales manager plans and carries out all company sales meetings, hires and trains salespeople, arranges and sometimes attends dealer meetings, and takes care of all details related to the sales staff.

## The Marketing Staff

The advertising department of a company works hand-in-hand with the sales organization to support and promote the acceptance of a company product.

The advertising manager prepares and submits for approval an advertising budget, usually for a 12-month fiscal period, then tries to spend the available funds in the most effective manner. In these days of massive advertising programs sponsored by such industries as automobile and appliance manufacturers, even a large expenditure by an instrument manufacturer would seem minuscule by comparison.

The advertising manager is also responsible for collateral materials describing the products used by retailers in their daily customer contacts, including catalogs, folders, specifications, service and operating manuals, banners, signs, etc. He supervises all media advertising in newspapers, educational journals, magazines and on radio and television.

Some companies maintain a complete advertising department and are equipped to handle all in-house requirements. The majority, however, have a limited staff and use an independent advertising agency for both creative talent and service assistance.

As an adjunct of the advertising department, a few companies maintain a program of public relations, also carried out by an outside firm specializing in such work.

The combination of sales, advertising and promotion is collectively called "marketing." A marketing manager or director has overall responsibility for developing and coordinating a long-range marketing plan. Generally, the better the planning, the more successful the company.

## Other Personnel Areas

Especially important to a manufacturing plant is the service department, staffed by experts who are thoroughly familiar with the product. The service staff handles any problems with the product, gives advice and instruction, and sends replacement parts when needed. Staffers deal with retailers, jobbers, wholesalers, distributors, independent technicians and owners of both old and new instruments.

The musical instrument manufacturing industry, like any other business, relies on a number of departments to make operations run smoothly. These include personnel, purchasing, payroll, credit and accounting.

Educational requirements for the various jobs described in this section vary according to the individual assignment responsibilities. Generally, a high school degree is necessary for clerks and typists, and additional education for bookkeeping, secretarial and statistical work. Most upper-level jobs require a college degree.

Despite the sophistication so often observed in today's business organizations, there is still every opportunity for the person starting at the bottom of the ladder in whatever capacity to aspire and ultimately attain the top position.

# Careers in Wholesaling

For the business-minded music student who likes selling but doesn't want to go into retailing or manufacturing, there is another career possibility: wholesaling.

The wholesaler is a liaison between the manufacturer and the retailer. He buys large quantities of instruments, sheet music and accessories and resells to smaller music merchants who may want anything from a single bass to a gross of self-instruction aids, a dozen violin strings to 1,000 harmonicas.

Wholesalers supply large and small retailers who may not be able to buy directly from a manufacturer. They also import instruments in quantities large enough to make them competitively priced for consumer resale.

As in most businesses, wholesalers have a sales force assigned to specific territories. These territories might encompass several states with hundreds of retailers which the salesmen visit on a regular basis, taking orders for merchandise and displaying new products.

Since wholesalers buy in larger quantities then they sell at any given time, there are beginning jobs in the warehousing and inventory operations including stock clerks, packers and shippers and order takers.

Some wholesalers also manufacture small instruments in their own facilities or may be the exclusive importer for instruments manufactured abroad to their own specifications. These are often sold under an exclusive brand by the wholesaler.

In addition, there are opportunities for advertising specialists including artists and copywriters. Many wholesalers also have their own service staff to repair and maintain the instruments catalogued. Some wholesalers, who do not have their own service staff, will have access to repairmen in their own community who can do the necessary service work.

Wholesalers are located throughout the country, although those that specialize in imported instruments are located near the two coasts.

Salaries for the various job classifications are about equal to those for similar jobs in other industries in the wholesalers' area. Pay scales for the sales staff tend to be somewhat higher than those in retail sales but depend on the abilities of the individual salesman, the size of the territory and the number of retailers serviced.

Educational requirements also match those for similar jobs in other industries. While a salesman does not need to play an instrument well, he should know the products he sells, their capabilities and limitations.

Wholesaling is one of the most diversified and fastest growing aspects of the music business and has excellent opportunities for the person seeking a challenging business career.

# Careers in Music Publishing

Music publishing is a multifaceted field composed of interdependent operations, each involving a specific career opportunity.

The publishing process begins with the selection of what will be published—whether it's an original musical composition or a new arrangement of an existing composition.

In some firms, the selection is handled by the director of publications, who may also serve as an editor. His qualifications almost defy description, since the work calls for highly developed musical taste, a strong sense of the market and an eye on the budget.

Sometimes it's the sole function of the director of Publications to accept, reject or commission a work; sometimes the decision is made by a committee, and in other instances, by the head of the music publishing company.

Once the work is accepted for publication, it must be readied for production. An editor reviews the manuscript and makes sure that everything is in perfect order, from the proper spelling of the title to the last dynamic mark on the page.

When the editor completes his work, the manuscript moves on to a music engraver, a music typographer or an autographer. An engraver puts the notes down in the style familiar to all musicians by etching the music out of a soft metal plate with special tools. The typographer accomplishes the same task by using a typewriter; the autographer writes music by hand. Some of the people engaged in this work create quite excellent artistic music notations.

The engraved plates, typed or autographed pages must be proofread. Sometimes the composer himself handles this task, but more frequently it's the function of a professional proofreader who makes certain that the music conforms to the manuscript.

The work is then returned to the engraver who carries out the changes. It is given one final check by the proofreader.

With the music completed, an artist designs the cover and adds any necessary sketches or photographs. The work is now ready for the printer.

The background and training of composers, editors and proofreaders is very similar. Although a composer's area of expertise may vary from a proofreader's, both should have as broad a background in all areas of music as possible. Understanding of composition and arranging processes, of proper notation of music, of style and of form related to all types of music is a must.

Although many editors specialize, the broader your base of knowledge the better  because the opportunities are much greater if you're well versed in all musical styles.

For example, if you have an understanding of contemporary and popular music as well as the classics, you'll generally be more appealing to a potential employer than if your scope of understanding is limited to pre-1920 music.

There are, however, situations which call for a specialist: a person with an extensive general background coupled with a specific area of expertise, e.g., keyboard music of the baroque era. If you'd like to specialize—as an editor, composer or arranger—it would be to your advantage to acquire a solid general background before concentrating on a specific area.

If you're interested in becoming an engraver/typographer/autographer, artist or printer, an understanding of music is helpful, but is not absolutely necessary. You will probably be trained on the job in an apprentice-type manner, or through a special school or instruction program.

After the composition is printed, the next step is to let the public know about it. This is the responsibility of the advertising professionals.

If you'd like to specialize in the promotion of music publications through advertising, you'll need special training in this field. Although it's not essential to have musical training, it is necessary to understand the nature of the publications from the vantage point of the consuming musician.

**Specialized Areas**

While these career opportunities are typical throughout the entire music publishing field, there are also a number of other specialized areas:

*Standard publishing includes master works, special editions and publications of past and present serious music.*

*Educational publishing concentrates on both instructional and performance material for preschool to college levels.*

*Popular music publishing revolves around current songs and standards [those which maintain their popularity after their initial success].*

Further career opportunities exist in music promotion. Some companies specializing in music for use in schools employ lecturers and clinicians to maintain contact with educators who are potential customers.

Companies that publish concert music, ballets and operas naturally try to encourage the performance of such works. Stimulating such performances may, in a few instances, be the responsibility of a full-time employee; more often, however, it is an additional responsibility of someone engaged in other activities within the organization.

In popular music publishing, a key role is played by the professional manager whose responsibilities vary from company to company. Generally, however, managers are in charge of acquiring new songs, arranging for their recording and promoting their performance on radio and television.

The professional manager may be assisted by one or more promotion people who work with radio disc jockeys to stimulate broadcast exposure.

Although most publishing firms employ outside counsel for complex legal problems, there is a continuing need for a copyright department manager—an in-house employee with a good working knowledge of copyright procedures and implications for the music publishing business.

Much of this knowledge can be obtained through on-the-job training, familiarity with copyright law, the procedures of the U.S. Copyright Office, protection of rights throughout the world and other aspects of copyright.

Closely identified with the copyright department manager, and frequently the same person, is the rights and permissions manager. This job involves the licensing of copyrights of the company's music for use in recordings, motion pictures, television films, commercials and arrangements for publication by others.

Here, too, on-the-job training is the general rule. But you can get briefed on the subject through a music business course.

The National Association of Recording Arts and Sciences (NARAS) Institute maintains a file on music business courses including those on copyright. For further information, write to the NARAS Institute, 505 North Lake Shore Drive, Suite 6505, Chicago, Illlinois 60611.

Music publishing is, comparatively speaking, a small business. Getting started is largely a matter of determining what career aspect is particularly interesting, then knocking on doors.

While there are music publishing companies rather broadly scattered around the country, the center for standard music publishing has traditionally been the New York metropolitan area. Other areas for popular music publishing are Los Angeles and Nashville.

The National Music Publishers Assn. recently started an employment referral service for its members. The service provides a comprehensive outline of various job categories in music publishing which do not require a knowledge of music.

**Where Do You Fit?**

If you were knowledgeable in all these areas, could you do everything yourself? Well, that's how many people begin in publishing. An individual with a love of music and its presentation in printed form is the potential future publisher.

This type of person is often a specialist in a specific field and has a point of view that he wants to convey to others. He starts by publishing in this field, performing all of the functions previously discussed. As the business expands, others are hired and trained to handle specific functions in the overall production. One can easily see, therefore, that some business background is also a necessity.

Music publishing offers a unique opportunity to begin your own business. It is one of the few business areas that offers possibilities for the individual working almost completely on his own to make things happen for himself and for the people who write and perform music.

Morton Manus
National Music Publishers Assn.

# Careers in Piano Tuning

# Careers in Piano Tuning

A piano tuner-technician tunes, regulates the mechanism to optimum performance, and makes necessary repairs or replacements of parts on pianos. Most of the work is performed in homes because that is where most pianos are located. Technicians also work in schools, conservatories, studios, churches, concert halls, music stores and piano rebuilding shops.

Most piano tuner-technicians are independent, relying for business on their reputations and a clientele developed over a period of years. Some, however, work as regular employees of, or on contract with, schools and music stores. Although traditionally man's work, the field is more and more attracting women who find the work satisfying and a convenient match with household responsibilities.

Besides learning the skills involved in developing proficiency, an independent piano tuner-technician must be personable and capable of personal and business discipline in order to be successful.

Tuning is an acquired skill, not at all related to musical talent or ability to identify pitches. First, your ear must be trained to hear the interferences (called beats) caused by two nearly identical frequencies of sound; second, your mind must be trained to know how to use the speed of beats to establish "equal temperament," based usually on a mechanical pitch source of standard frequency like a tuning fork; and finally, coordination must be developed between the ear and the hand manipulating the tuning lever, to accomplish minute adjustments of tension in each of a piano's 225-odd strings.

Learning this process and achieving proficiency in it takes time and practice, similar in many respects to learning to play the instrument. Electronic frequency-comparison devices have been developed in recent years that can be an aid in learning and practice, but they do not substitute for the judgemental factor required of the trained ear in dealing with pianos having varying degrees of inharmonicity.

While the theory of tuning can be learned by correspondence course or from a book, a significant amount of personal instruction interspersed with practice is required for achieving correct results. Although individuals differ somewhat, a learning period of at least two years is needed for most persons to be able to tune acceptably.

In contrast to the typical piano tuner of years ago who usually had only enough knowledge of the mechanics of a piano to make silent notes play or to patch broken parts, the modern piano tuner-technician learns to fine-regulate the piano "action" and keys to factory specifications using a variety of special tools.

Breakage or malfunction of parts of newer pianos is usually handled by parts replacement and reregulation. But if new parts aren't readily available, such as for older pianos or when working in remote areas, the tuner-technician must have the ability to make or adapt parts that will function correctly. Both the piano student and the accomplished musician have a right to expect their tuner-technician to maintain instruments at optimum levels of mechanical and musical performance. Again, while much can be learned about piano mechanism from reading and study, only actual practice under supervision in a residence school, a piano shop, or by an independent tuner-technician will assure progress to a satisfactory level of competence.

Piano tuner-technicians frequently specialize in particular kinds of piano work. Such specialties might concentrate on keyboard repair, concert and studio piano maintenance (usually possible only in metropolitan areas), or restoration of antique instruments. Not all of these specialties require the ability to tune.

Some larger public school systems, and many universities and colleges, have piano tuner-technicians as full-time staff members. The schools provide shop space, tools and materials, and the regular hours and fringe benefits usual to such institutions. Because these positions offer almost automatic prestige and security not so easily achieved in independent practice, salaries may be somewhat less than a well-established person can earn on his own. However, because of the demands of music school faculties, standards for these positions are usually quite high.

In certain areas of the country, particularly the South and East, many music stores employ piano tuner-technicians to do piano service in homes, for which the employee may receive a salary and travel allowance, or a commission. In these situations the store performs the management functions of taking calls and arranging appointments as well as collecting fees from customers. The employed tuner-technician may enjoy fringe benefits he would otherwise have to provide for himself plus an assured income, but his standards of performance and potential earnings will be dictated by his employer.

In addition, the employed person may at times be required to do work in the store which is below his level of training and competence just in order to be busy. However, working in a store is an excellent way to develop proficiency and gain experience prior to starting an independent practice.

The personal freedom and independence possible for a well-trained piano tuner-technician, combined with the near-professional relationship with clientele and the satisfaction of combining intellect and hand to recreate beauty is attracting many young men and women into the field.

While success depends on many factors, the fact remains that as long as there are pianos, piano tuner-technicians will be needed. Persons with the capacity and determination to excel in the work may never get rich in dollars. Their wealth will lie in what they know and can do, without dependence on an employer and with little investment other than the time and effort of learning.

Earnings for a well-established independent piano tuner-technician working full time depend on local rates and time spent traveling to jobs. Of the total earnings, about 40% would go for operating expenses, overhead, taxes, insurance and provisions for education and retirement.

Piano tuner-technicians are not "regulated" or licensed, but pressure for such controls could increase in the future as a natural outgrowth of consumer demand for protection from unethical and incompetent persons who too often take advantage of the public's limited knowledge.

Meanwhile, voluntary associations are active in establishing standards of professional competence and conduct.

James H. Burton
Piano Technicians Guild

# RECORDING

The information in this chapter was
compiled with the assistance of:

Stanley M. Gortikov, Recording
Industry Association of America

Walter Hurst, author-attorney

Leo de Gar Kulka, president,
College for Recording Arts

Goddard Lieberson, composer, critic,
former president of Columbia Records

Charles Suber, president,
National Academy of Recording Arts
and Sciences [NARAS] Institute

# Careers in the Recording Industry

# Careers in the Recording Industry

The lure of music, the mystique surrounding recording artists and musicians, the stereotyped fantasies of "show biz" have encouraged a good deal of interest in the record business as a career.

Despite the high sales and high visibility of aspects of recording, job opportunities are not abundant. In fact, 75% of all records released don't even recover their costs. Not only are jobs relatively scarce, the financial liabilities of the business are great.

Yes, some men and women find fulfillment of their dreams but most do not. There is no formula to "break into" the business nor is there one technique that will allow you to zoom ahead of competitors.

While there are several centers for recording in this country—Los Angeles, New York, Chicago, Nashville, San Francisco, Memphis and Atlanta—there are recording studios throughout the United States and often your chances of getting that "first break" are better in a less competitive community.

The record industry is fragmented: It consists of some very large organizations and hundreds of small ones, some with a very short life span.

If you want to enter the business of producing and selling records, talk to other people who are already in the recording industry—in record stores, record companies, studios, anywhere a staff member can be helpful in separating fact from myth.

Regardless of which recording industry specialty you eventually want to pursue, there are some skills and personal attributes that are basic:

- A working knowledge of music—including theory, arranging and composition.

- Flexibility in adapting your talents to all kinds of music.

- Reliability in meeting deadlines and commitments.

All recordings of popular music start with a song—either one written for a specific artist or a "standard" that has been arranged in a new way.

Some songwriters work through a publisher; others publish their own works. Songs can be brought to the attention of performers, recording companies or "A&R"* men by publishing companies or by the songwriters themselves.

Careers in composing and publishing are more fully reviewed in separate chapters (see pages 31 and 80).

Following are descriptions of jobs directly related to the actual production and distribution of a record.

**The Record Producer and A&R Man** may be employed by a record company, by an artist, or work as an "independent." He is the liaison between the publisher, the artist and the record company, matching songs with artists and musicians to produce a commercially successful sound.

Duties include finding new artists as well as fresh material for established singers and groups; hiring arrangers and copyists as needed; preparing the recording session budget, and getting authorization to spend money or raise funds from outside sources.

The producer will then work with an engineer to create the vocal and instrumental combination that he thinks will sell records.

Major recording companies hire A&R specialists who have proven themselves successful producers and demonstrate a talent for creating best sellers. Consequent advancement in this area of the recording business depends on the ability—quite literally—to produce results at the point of sale.

To get production experience you may want to consider working with a promising band that would like to try making a record. Sometimes a group's personal manager will raise money for a recording session and "A&R" it.

Occasionally, an arranger or conductor will insist on handling the production duties to ensure that the music is recorded as written.

Songwriters and publishers also have an opportunity to produce when they record demonstration records or tapes.

*Artist and Repertoire

# Careers in the Recording Industry

**The Studio Arranger**, whether freelance or affiliated with a particular studio, has the job of scoring the song for the group and the instruments to be used during the recording session. The arranger may be a songwriter scoring his own works, a member of a performing group or work full-time at arranging. Arranger's fees are set by union contracts based on number of score pages. The more scores an arranger prepares, the higher his wages. Many arrangers work nights, when there are no disturbances from phone calls or drop-in visitors. Daytime hours are spend answering inquiries and sometimes conducting.

If you want to become an arranger, it is important that you learn how to read music swiftly and write neatly. While you don't have to play any instruments well, it is imperative that you have a working knowledge of each instrument for which you might be scoring, including their timbres, temperaments and ranges. You need a good sense of what's currently popular and an instinct for future trends.

**The Copyist** transcribes the arranger's score for each musician or group of instruments. He may be hired directly by a record company or by the master producer, the arranger or the music department of a film or television production company.

Hours are highly irregular. A copyist is usually given 12 hours work for a recording session about 12 hours before the scheduled session to prepare the manuscripts for each studio musician.

Fees are set by union contract and vary depending on amount of music, type of instrument as well as type of paper used.

To become a copyist, you must be able to read music and to write legibly, rapidly and accurately. A knowledge of musical theory and harmony is helpful.

As a copyist, you will become acquainted with a great deal of music written for the commercial market and will have the chance to meet many influential people in the recording business.

Many copyists often move on to careers as arrangers.

**The Music Contractor** steps in after the A&R man has decided on the instrumental and vocal complement for a recording session. The union contractor checks to see that all the musicians to be called are members of the American Federation of Musicians (AFofM) and that vocalists are members of the American Federation of Television and Radio Artists (AFTRA).

At the session, the union contractor is the expert on union rules and settles any problems which might arise. He will make sure that each participant receives income tax deduction forms and that a report is filed with the AFofM and AFTRA on the hours worked and the personnel involved.

To quality as a union contractor, you must be a musician and a member of the union. You must be familiar with contract rules and regulations, the performance capabilities and specialties of various musicians in your area and the music preferences of the different A&R men.

Hours are highly irregular since the union contractor sets the session during business hours and then sits in when recordings are made.

Some contractors may also participate in the session as musicians. Therefore, a musician may want to look for producers who are willing to appoint him union contractor.

**The Musician Leader** organizes the singers, instrumentalists and background vocalists into one performing group. Frequently the leader may also write the arrangements and conduct.

Leaders make sure that the musicians perform well and within the time allocated for the recording session. They are paid double the scale of a musician.

Several leaders have risen from the ranks of studio musicians while others are arranger-conductors. Occasionally, the musician-leader may also serve as the session's union contractor.

**Recording Musicians/Sidemen** play in most recording sessions unless a symphony orchestra or the cast and orchestra of a Broadway play is to be featured.

Without exception, recording musicians are highly skilled professionals who can sight read music and normally give the A&R man, arranger, songwriter or conductor the right sounds on the first try. Delays at recording sessions are very expensive and are avoided as much as possible.

Sometimes sidemen will suggest routine or inventive changes, but arguments about arrangements are not tolerated. The recording musician must be able to cooperate fully, regard-less of personal musical style or taste.

Preparing for a career as a studio musician means developing good performance skills so that you can play almost any kind of music after reading the score.

To gain experience, participate in school musical ensembles, join with friends in groups or play in family get-togethers. Study music in college.

To gain entry in the field, start visiting recording studios, record companies, publishers, songwriters, in short, anyone who might be hiring musicians. Leave a business card on the chance that there might be a job for you.

Sometimes, arrangers and contractors may find their first-choice musicians unavailable and may call on friends or business associates as substitute sidemen.

On rare occasions sidemen have been hired while visiting a session when the A&R man decides to add a variation to the original arrangement. If the sideman shows potential, he may be called again on a future session.

Be available and let people know you are available.

**The Recording Engineer/Mixer** sets up the microphones and operates the equipment necessary to record the session in ac-cordance with the instructions of the A&R man.

The producer may give presession instructions to the engineer including a studio floor plan showing the instrumental groupings, placement of microphones and the screens to be used.

During the recording session, the A&R man will concentrate on listening to the music being played. The recording engineer concentrates on reproducing that sound on the equipment available, making adjustments requested by the producer. He may stop, start and play back several sets of tapes at the same time depending on whether the recording is monaural, stereo track, two-track, 16-track or more.

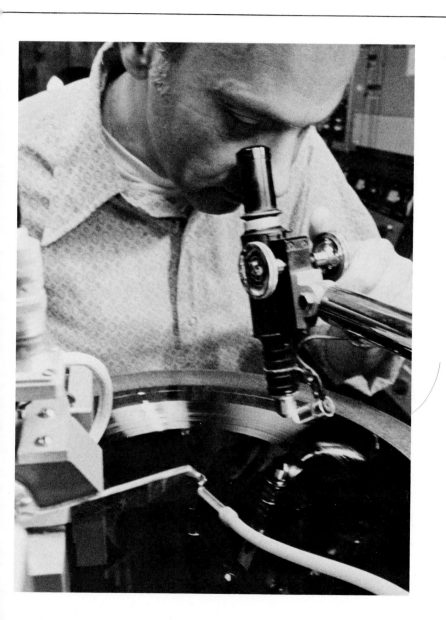

The engineer is concerned with five areas: musical range, rhythm, variety, dynamics and spectral control. The engineer must be able to compensate for limitations of the studio, the recording medium and the reproduction equipment.

Since engineering is one of the most popular career areas in recording, studios have become extremely selective in hiring.

To prepare yourself, enroll in a college that offers specific courses in sound engineering and learn how to operate all the technical machines, read the trade magazines and visit recording studios.

Try to get a job in a studio to learn more about the capabilities of the equipment around you. One well-known engineer started as a studio maintenance man. He worked with the equipment while repairing it and eventually moved up to an engineering spot.

For all the jobs outlined above, master your chosen craft and get to know people already in the field. That's the surest way to get a job.

Once you get experience, getting a job with a major record company or in a big city recording center becomes less difficult.

## The Business Side of Recording

In addition to creating and producing records, the recording industry offers many job opportunities that are on the business side. Often these jobs give valuable insights into what makes a record a success.

**Selling** the completed record directly to retailers and to wholesalers in a given geographic area is one of the best ways to learn the record business.

You might be called upon to appraise product requirements, take orders, introduce new records, evaluate stock, merchandise the product and arrange for advertising and merchandising programs. Sales people often start as part of the junior sales staff, as order or inventory clerks. Sales personnel may work directly for record companies or for independent distributors or rack jobbers.

**Merchandising** is a sales-support function within a record company. It includes developing programs of communication to help sell the product. Merchandising includes responsibility for advertising, display, customer communications, sales staff communication and sales literature.

**Promotion** in the record industry usually is geared toward radio and television. Duties are devoted to maximizing airplay of the record. This is done through personal contact with management and broadcast personnel.

**Graphics** are important to the recording business for packaging, display work and merchandising units. An entire graphics industry is peripheral to the recording business and many opportunities are available in this related field.

**Manufacturing** jobs vary from unskilled labor to skilled production work and sophisticated control and management responsibilities. Not all record companies manufacture their own records and tapes, but thousands of jobs of all kinds are open around the country to meet the production requirements of the industry.

**General Management** involves the various levels of administrative and executive jobs filled by generalists and specialists in the industry. Most of these people come up through the ranks by demonstrating unusual skills.

One important fact to bear in mind about the recording industry is that it is oriented to "smallness" rather than "bigness." In almost every job category mentioned there are individuals and small independent enterprises that "go it alone." Often these represent the best opportunities for a newcomer to break into the field and eventually become an entrepreneur.

The very nature of records also fragments many of the functions into product types. There are often different companies or departments within a company which produce classical, rock, country-western, soul, ethnic or spoken word records.

**The Disc Jockey** combines the skills of a lively commentator with a knowledge of current musical trends and the technical ability to operate the equipment in the broadcasting studio.

# Careers in the Recording Industry

Air play by a disc jockey can have a profound and far-reaching effect on record sales.

The "DJ" schedules music, prepares "ad lib" introductions for commercials, conducts quizzes and contests and sometimes produces spot announcements for the radio station.

At larger stations the DJ may work with the music director or program manager to select music in keeping with the station's format—middle-of-the-road, young adult and contemporary, "golden oldies" or preteen rock. Or the DJ may have a show that appeals to a specific segment of the station's general audience —teens, housewives, country fans, etc.

The DJ may have the services of an engineer during regular office hours but be required to do his own technical work in the early morning or late evening hours.

Since disc jockeys try to develop a personal following to maintain high audience ratings for the station, they frequently make free or paid appearances at sponsors' places of business, dances, record hops, clubs and other promotional events where they can meet the public and their fans.

If you want to become a disc jockey, it is important to combine your music studies with courses in English and public speaking. Take radio courses in your high school if they are available and, of course, in college.

Visit local radio stations to see the disc jockey at work. The best time to visit stations is before and after business hours when a disc jockey may be more willing to talk to you and show you how everything works.

Learn all you can about the artists and songs currently popular by listening to records and the radio. Study the styles of disc jockeys so that you can develop one suited to your personality. Practice by working at your school's station, and by acting as master of ceremonies at school dances and record hops. Programming records for school social events is good experience for radio programming.

Be sure to tape your appearances for later playback so that you can analyze your own performance.

After you've graduated and are ready for a job, try the smaller stations first. You may also have more leeway in music scheduling and programming at a smaller station. One California-based DJ, whose show is syndicated around the country, started on a local station where he had the opportunity to play his favorite novelty records. The show became so popular that he moved to a larger station and eventually began to tape the program for replay.

**The Music Industry Attorney** is a specialist in copyright structure, restrictions on publications, mechanical reproductions and performance rights licensing.

He understands union agreements as well as terms and conditions of publisher contracts, problems of independent master producers, record and tape distribution and methods of accounting as well as record and tape retailing, promotional practices, artist and manager agreements and the problems and potentials of the video cassette.

In addition, the same music industry attorneys handle all the nonmusic business and personal legal matters of their clients.

Naturally you must become a lawyer first, but if you want to specialize in music, it helps to learn the business early.

There is no "right way" for you to get started in any of these jobs. Knock on doors. Be persistent. Be creative. Be direct and simple in your resumes but don't overlook creative ways to enter a creative business.

Research before you look and think before you talk.

You can be frustrated by the cliches you will hear about not having experience. But remember that at some point every individual now working in the industry had to get experience. Unfortunately, the industry employs few part-timers and summer occupations are few and far between.

Training requirements for each of the jobs are different because different skills are needed. Many of the positions are taught only on the job. For specific guidance, try to meet with a specialist now employed in the particular field in which you are interested. Ask for counsel as to the preparation that would be most helpful to you in attaining your career ambitions.

Stanley M. Gortikov
Recording Industry Association
of America

Walter Hurst
Attorney-author

Leo de Gar Kulka,
College for Recording Arts

Charles Suber
NARAS Institute

# ALLIED FIELDS

The information in the chapters which
follow was compiled with the
assistance of :

Lee H. Bristol, Jr., president
emeritus, Westminster Choir College

Richard Freed, Music Critics Assn.

Thom Jones, Fellowship of
United Methodist Musicians

Richard J. Schuler, editor, *Sacred Music*

Margaret S. Sears, National
Association for Music Therapy

Susan T. Sommer, Music Library Assn.

# Careers in Church Music

# Careers in Church Music

Careers in church music can be almost as numerous and varied as churches and synagogues themselves, but such career opportunities seem to have in common the fact that they provide a rewarding chance to lead others in music-making and to help the church through music to enrich people's lives.

Just as denominations differ, even churches within a given denomination can differ markedly from one another. Size, locale, resources, traditions and even competition can make job opportunities in one parish as different as day and night from those in another.

There may be job opportunities for a full-time director of music who has overall responsibility for all the music in a given church and such a job may call for an assistant to serve as his or her organist. In other churches, both large and small (and this is particularly true of Episcopal churches), the organist and choirmaster may be one person who may have an assistant depending on the size and budget of the parish. In some churches, responsibility for music may be vested in persons who must perform dual functions. Director of music might be combined with youth work, for example, or education, or business management, or even director of creative arts where music will be only one aspect of the job.

Salaries are usually higher for these combination jobs but may require a broad background for both functions to be handled well.

The musician who serves as director of music and youth work, for example, must not only have the music background described above but an understanding of young people as well. Such a dual job may require a person not only to have a thorough grasp of vocal and instrumental music but an understanding of dramatics and dancing as well.

The musician who serves as director of music and education will, of course, have to add to his music background a thorough grounding in the basics of religious education and how to plan and direct programs for both young and old.

The musician who doubles as music director and business manager will need to learn the basics of management. Many a church musician in such a dual job finds the two assignments provide a refreshing "change of pace."

The director of creative arts is a relatively new job combining music with a program that involves all the arts—dance, drama, graphic arts, etc. Such jobs are rare today and involve a broad grasp of many disciplines.

What qualifications should an applicant have for a career in church music? At the outset, you will need talent and technique, of course, but you will also need to have the drive and self-discipline to put that ability to work. Above and beyond ability and drive, the church musician will need to be sure he or she has the capacity to handle the human relations involved, for the church musician has to draw music from many people and work well with them.

A choir director today needs a thorough understanding of music fundamentals, including a knowledge of harmony, theory, counterpoint, the human voice, choral and instrumental conducting, a basic keyboard facility, choral and organ repertoire old and new, as well as liturgics, hymnody and history. Whether you plan to serve a Roman Catholic or Protestant church, it will be important to understand all traditions from Gregorian chant to rock music of the present day.

An organist today—and America's standards among performing organists have never been higher—should have an understanding of the instrument and its literature as well as technique and repertoire. It will be important for the organist to remember that recital or solo-playing, leading a congregation in the singing of hymns and canticles, and accompanying choirs and soloists each require different skills. It is possible for a gifted recitalist to be a poor service player and vice versa. One needs to have a "feel" for worship in order for one's music to enrich worship, lift it above the limitations of mere language, and perhaps tie together different parts of a service.

If an organist can develop the ability to improvise, this can be an important asset. Up to a point this ability can be developed in almost any organist, although some are bound to have greater skills in this area than others. Outside of progressive jazz, there is probably no area where improvisation can be used to such advantage.

If you entertain thoughts of one day entering the field of church music, you will do well to involve yourself in as many musical activities as possible in high school. You will want to take private vocal and instrumental lessons where possible, sing in a school choral group and maybe your local church choir. You will do well to seek opportunities to try conducting others and maybe playing in an instrumental ensemble. In all you do musically try to develop your sense of rhythm and pitch and try to train your ears really to "hear" musical sounds and detect subtle differences in the music to which you listen.

After high school, you may wish to choose a college or university or a music school specializing in church music. You will do well, in any case, to further your preparation with music and general courses you feel are related to the demands you may expect of a career in church music. It is important to try to gain practical experience in leading or accompanying music in actual services. Many colleges not only offer but require such field experience as a part of the church music curriculum. Such field experience sometimes enables a student to earn a small salary while helping a church.

Your own education in church music and related subjects should continue even after formal schooling is completed. It is particularly important to keep abreast of what is going on in worship as well as the arts generally when so many churches are changing.

We are living in a day when liturgical churches are becoming more free-form and experimental in their worship and some of the more evangelical and traditionally free-form churches are becoming more formal and liturgical in their services. It is possible today to hear a Latin mass sung at a Unitarian Church in New York and attend an informal Roman Catholic service in Texas that is not unlike the kind of service one might expect to find in a Presbyterian church in Minnesota. It is important to keep abreast of what is going on not only in your own denomination but others as well, so that you can make a greater, more knowledgeable contribution to your own church.

Across the country there are countless workshops, seminars and courses to help you in your continuing education. In the late fall, church music journals begin listing these summer courses, giving you a chance to choose either general or specific programs you feel you need. Overseas, Britain's Royal School of Church Music offers a summer course specifically designed for Americans. This course helps a student learn firsthand from professional church musicians (cathedral organists and others) who must supply music for services seven days a week. (For information contact the Royal School of Church Music, Addington Palace, Croydon, Surrey, England.)

Church choral programs can vary all the way from a huge multiple-choir setup involving 1200 volunteer singers in one church (one can find a number of such churches in the Southwest today) to the sophisticated, paid men-and-boy choir program one often may find flourishing in an Eastern metropolitan or suburban church.

More and more these days, musicians seem to be veering away from an exclusive reliance on that four-part, choral-and-organ sound that has traditionally been associated with church. Happily, many new anthems and hymns call for unusual accompaniments or even no accompaniment at all. There is more use of unison singing, choir and congregational refrain songs, and far greater use of auxiliary instruments than in the past. Using auxiliary instruments not only provides variety and varied music textures but a chance to involve the instrumentalists in wonderful ways.

Many churches find that extra, purely musical programs can be rewarding and fun as well as a means of helping one's church make contact with people in the community it might initially reach in no other way.

In addition to regular services and extra musical programs for the community, the organist will have responsibility for other occasional services like weddings and funerals, which help to supplement his or her income.

Church budgets these days are limited, and job openings for full-time church musicians are also limited. But those who pursue full-time or even part-time careers in church music seem to find such work challenging and personally satisfying.

If you are interested in a career in church music, you will do well to talk to organists, choir directors and clergymen in your community. Their experience and advice can be invaluable in helping you chart your next steps.

Lee H. Bristol, Jr.
President emeritus
Westminster Choir College

Thom Jones
Fellowship of United
Methodist Musicians

Richard J. Schuler
Editor, *Sacred Music*

# Careers in Music Therapy

The use of music to influence changes in behavior is known as music therapy. It is a recognized treatment discipline for which educational preparation is required. Although it is often referred to as a recent addition to the health care field, its history can be traced back to the beginnings of recorded civilization. Music and healing have been entwined through most of man's existence. The functional role of music in most societies has been equal to, if not paramount to, its artistic role.

Music therapy employs music media directed by a trained music therapist to maintain, restore and improve mental and physical health. The basic treatment goal is to enable the individual to function more successfully within his specific environment. Music therapists work in psychiatric hospitals, mental retardation centers, physical disability hospitals and schools, community mental health centers, day care centers, nursing homes, special education schools and special services agencies.

The basic principles upon which appropriate music activities are constructed and behaviorial changes effected are applicable to many different treatment settings. The materials used and techniques employed are often transferable from one type of disability to another. Because music therapy is used in a wide variety of settings, it is a logical career choice for those interested in combining music with personal service.

Whether your interest lies with children or the aged, learning disabilities, emotional illness or behavior modification, music therapy is a recognized treatment used by many institutions which provide health services.

If you hope to become a music therapist, you should take every opportunity in high school to excel on your chosen instrument. You should also try to gain some experience conducting instrumental and vocal groups. You should be able to play piano, and by all means seek a teacher who is knowledgeable in this specialized teaching technique.

Proficiency on a number of instruments—such as guitar, ukulele, recorder, autoharp, ethnic and rhythm instruments—is required. You may want to buy several of these (most are relatively inexpensive) since you will use them regularly throughout your career.

# Careers in Music Therapy

To gain experience, you can begin your orientation to the basic hospital regimen by volunteering at a local institution. Some students find summer jobs working in institutions or at special camps for children with physical and mental disabilities.

College preparation in music therapy focuses predominantly on music and psychology. The student not only must demonstrate proficiency on his major instrument, but must also develop skill on a variety of instruments, such as guitar, accordion, recorder and others associated with folk music. While in college you will gain experience in clinical practices by observing and conducting activities at treatment facilities.

Following academic course work, you will complete a six-month clinical training internship at one of more than 80 approved treatment institutions. A standard baccalaureate music therapy curriculum, which includes the areas described above, has been developed by the National Association for Music Therapy, Inc., and is offered by 42 universities. Course work is required in the following areas:

**Music Therapy** — minimum of 10 semester hours

**Psychology or Educational Psychology** — 10-12 semester hours

**Sociology and Anthropology** — 6-8 semester hours

**Music** — 60 semester hours

**General Education** — 30 semester hours

**General Electives** — 6 semester hours

**Total** — 128 semester hours

The professional (music therapy) courses deal with the theory and practice of music therapy, and are taught by instructors who are competent in their field and who have a background in psychology as well.

A master's degree is offered at seven of the approved universities. The minimum requirement for those aspiring to enter music therapy teaching at the college level includes a master's degree plus clinical experience as a music therapist.

The field is not only growing quite rapidly, but is also undergoing marked changes. Not many years ago very few institutions except psychiatric hospitals included music therapy in their treatment programs. Gradually, as institutions of all types began examining the traditional forms of treatment offered, more experimentation with alternative modes of treatment was undertaken. Music therapy, one of those alternatives, is now found in a wide variety of institutions. This trend is expected to continue for some time.

Working conditions, of course, vary considerably depending on the nature of the institution or hospital and the number of patients involved. While music therapists work with a basic plan of therapy, adjustments or "improvisations" may be required for specific situations.

A therapist normally works in one institution with groups of patients—although it may be necessary to work with individuals on a one-to-one basis. Therapy schedules may range from several times a week with small groups to less frequent sessions with larger groups.

Salaries, too, vary with the size of the institution, its location and budget.

Margaret S. Sears
National Association for Music Therapy

# Careers in Music Criticism

**J Feather**

three or ...
phonists.

His treatment is long, si...
tour de force.

## Chicago composer worth reviving

**Paul Hume**

SHINGTON — Antal Do-
ecently conducted the Na-
Symphony Orchestra in
ormances of "Sky-
rs" by John Alden Car-
, whose 100th anniversa-
last Feb. 28.
ng Carpenter's music...

serving our Bicentennial, for
our 200th birthday should by
no means be limited to hearing
of new music that has been
and is still being written for
this anniversary year. It is
fully as important, particularly because we will have a lot
of catching up to do...

when that music did not often
receive cdial receptions
from our orchestral con-
ductors, and therefore from
their audiences.

It should be repeated
frequently that we have a vast
backlog of music written for
with the possible
opera, that should
t only this year

born two years
ves, is very like
land contempo-
spect. Ives' par-
posing with un-
ccess in the in-

was made vice president of the
company. In the meantime, he
studied theory in Chicago from
1908 to 1912. By then he felt
sure enough of himself to begin publishing what grew into
an impressive list of works.

There is a Concertino for piano and orchestra that has a
biting wit in its skilled writing.
An orchestral suite called "Ad-
ventures in a Perambulator"
had a wide success in the 1920s
and '30s, with its openly hu-
morous and realistic descriptions of nurses strolling with
baby carriages along the more
fashionable parts of...

## Solti's 7th seaso

Sir Georg Solti and the Chicago Symphony
Orchestra and Chorus venture once more

Its central theme is

## Bartok
## that bir

SIR GEORG SOLTI began his ...
... the Chicago Symphony Orchestra
campus concert in the University
Hall. The ancient auditorium ...
... symphony orchestra concert.

That portion of the ensemble sit
cenium loses its sound in the drape
stage strings are unduly promine
room to get all the players onstage
... is entirely ...

## Bowie et al

**Robinson**

debut fil...
Earth," h...
utor. Rus...
se the N...
throughou...
premiere s...
hile no Chi...
film opens...
Dallas and...

---

## Opera

## 'Pinafore' sails in sea of musical comedy

Joseph excels on all three counts. Less of
... either Peter Pratt or Mar-
... line and bit

## Supertramp rocks
## and eardrums roll

SUPERTRAMP: Roger Hodgson, guitar, keyboards, vocals; Rick Davies, keyboards, vocals; Dougie Thomson, bass;
John Helliwell, reeds keyboards; Bob C
Benberg, drums. Riviera Theater, Monday.

**By Al Rudis**

Those white flecks falling on
the audience and the B...
band Supertramp in...
iera Theater Mond...
were not some kind o
effect. They were bits
old building's plaster,
loose by the bone-r.
sound of the rock group.

Whoever decided ...

namics. Dynamics go out t
window when the sound is a
one uniform, deafening level.

Even so, the instr...
weren't affected...
in fact...

## Concert: A Sona

Professor of Viola and F
at Eastman School D

**Matre**

## enver smile
## uts a happy
## ace on others

...t you like about John Denver,
...Mountain high; other...

---

## Tempo/Entertainment

## Opry stars captivate
## Arie Crown slickers

## Schubert

**ael Davis**

you don't have to be
o like Levy's, a whole
of city slickers proved
hat you don't have to
south of the Mason-
like the good ol'
y music of Loretta
way Twitty and Billy
Craddock.
hough the Arie Crown

didn't exactly
flavor of the
Opry, the thous
tended Sunday's
evening perform
theless got a h
of home-cooked n
Craddock open
with what the la...

## The Tubes: Fuzzy
## rock 'n' shlock

## G PHIL OC

The critic's job is less easy to define than might be thought, particularly since universally accepted standards for this profession have not yet been codified. As a critic, it is not your purpose simply to give a "report card" to performing musicians, but to make a meaningful contribution to the art that nurtures them and at the same time help expand the active audience by writing about music in a way that shows it as the vital and stimulating experience it is.

The specific duties of a music critic may vary from one publication to another, depending on the size of the staff and of the community. A large newspaper in a large community may have a staff of music specialists assigned to such fields as opera, early music, experimental music, etc., and critics who review recordings but not "live" events.

On smaller newspapers, the single critic will not only be expected to cover all musical events, both "live" and recorded, but may also be required to cover drama, dance, films and / or visual and plastic arts. In addition to actual reviewing, most critics (as differentiated from reviewers) are expected to editorialize occasionally or periodically (the Sunday or weekend "think piece") on events of unusual importance, the state of the art, problems of survival within the musical community, etc.

Irving Kolodin, one of America's most respected senior critics, has suggested that criticism "should start out with a basic understanding between the critic and the person being criticized; they should talk the same language." The critic should definitely have musical training, and, on the question of how much, Kolodin observes that "no amount is undesirable."

"The fundamental problem," he points out, is that the selection of critics is "generally slanted toward writers who know more or less about music, instead of toward musicians who know more or less about writing." Most respected critics agree that the critic should be a knowledgeable musician capable of expressing himself, rather than merely a skilled wordsmith with a smattering of musical knowledge.

# Careers in Music Criticism

For several years, the Rockefeller Foundation sponsored a series of seminars in criticism at the University of Southern California—designed not strictly for beginners, but for younger and less experienced professionals. There has been no regular, recognized graduate or undergraduate program in criticism at any university or conservatory.

The Music Critics Association, Inc., the professional organization of U.S. and Canadian critics, considers the education of critics and the establishment of recognized standards to be among its prime objectives; the association has been sponsoring summer institutes and workshops for critics in cooperation with music festivals and universities for several years, and is in contact with a number of colleges and universities regarding possibilities of creating a degree program in criticism.

Kolodin, who recommends a required course in criticism for every music student in his first year simply as part of his general background, emphasizes that the critic should follow that profession because he wants to be a critic, just as others want to be pianists or singers. "The unfortunate thing about criticism," he says, "is that it is usually a refuge rather than an objective."

Boris Nelson, music critic of the *Toledo Blade* and immediate past president of the Music Critics Association, offers this list of requirements for the aspiring critic:

1. A thorough musical background, historical and practical—i.e., theoretical knowledge and at least a basic knowledge of instrumentation, with actual ability to play an instrument.

2. A good ear—good genetically, but also trained and tuned.

3. Ability to write clearly and to the point—for the readership of a specific journal.

4. Constant listening and writing, augmented by general reading in the arts, history and the world-at-large.

5. Ability to identify personal preferences and dislikes as such, and to separate them from judgment-making in the interest of objectivity.

6. Involvement: a love for things musical, a high degree of enthusiasm and even idealism which communicates itself to the reader.

7. Willingness to stand up for a justifiable opinion, supported by knowledge, fairness and experience.

In short, it might be said that most of all you need passion for music, the drive to communicate it and the skill to make yourself understood. At the same time, you need the self-discipline to be dispassionate in your judgments. Ideally, the critic should write with such conviction and enthusiasm for the art (if not for every respective experience) as to make the reader who has never been particularly moved by music think "What have I been missing!"—and with such assurance and clarity as to inspire the confidence of the most sophisticated reader. You should never write "down" to the former group, and never be so foolish as to try to impress the latter with technical displays that could be of interest only to fellow critics and scholars.

Realistically, it must be said that this field is not expanding at the moment. Several major journals have cut back on their general coverage of the arts; some have ceased publication. Newspaper and magazine publishing has been one of the hardest hit segments of the economy. One possible entree is to make yourself "visible" in a related activity—e.g., broadcasting, program annotation, public relations work for musical organizations.

A more direct way, of course, is to apply for a position as assistant or "junior" critic with a newspaper or magazine with a large enough staff to include such positions, or to apply for "stringer" status. ("Stringers" are persons who are not members of the staff, but who are called in on an "as needed" basis to review a particular event.)

Junior critics, assistants and "stringers" are frequently the first to get the nod when a bigger job opens up, either on their own publication or another one.

Another avenue to employment as a critic is the establishment of your name through freelance articles and reviews. Such pieces may be submitted "on spec" ("on speculation," with no guarantee of acceptance) at first. Once you demonstrate your writing and criticism ability you may be invited to cover specific events. Several critics are quite active as freelancers, augmenting their earnings with jobs as teachers, program annotators, or in some entirely unrelated field. Few "make it" on freelance criticism alone.

Once in on the ground floor of a large-scale operation, the young critic would find himself doing chores for senior colleagues—for example, preparing the daily or weekly calendar of musical events, preparing the details of time, place, titles and personnel to accompany the senior critic's major review, keeping the schedule of department assignments, obtaining pictures for use with reviews. These duties serve to acquaint the "junior" critic with the importance of these details, which the critic on a smaller paper—or in a one-man department anywhere—must look after personally.

Interviews are also part of the critic's scope of operation which means he must be familiar with the work, outlook and personality of significant figures in music. The ability to be entertaining in such writing—as well as in the reviews themselves—is a substantial asset, so long as it is kept in reasonable proportion to the main objective.

Harold C. Schonberg, the music critic of *The New York Times* and winner of the first Pulitzer Prize awarded to a music critic, once observed that, in music, there are only two places one might find oneself: "New York—and out-of-town." More jobs and job possibilities exist in new York than in all the rest of America—but more applicants are after them in New York, too.

In other communities, there may be only a single newspaper, and that one may have one individual covering music, films, theater and gardening. If you find yourself in such a situation, you ought not to overlook the possibilities of writing and speaking on musical events, records, etc., for the local educational or "good music" radio station—and at the same time undertake to get your name known in larger areas via the freelance route.

Even the most successful critics cannot expect financial rewards anything like those realized by persons making similar commitments of themselves in industry or in several other professions. They can, however, enjoy a feeling of considerable fulfillment—not in terms of finding themselves recognized in a restaurant or having reviews quoted, but in helping to inform and stimulate both laymen and musicians among their readers.

A critic's ideas can help to expand the repertory of the performer—and that of the concert-goer and record-collector. The research a critic does (or ought to do) in preparing to write about a major performance or recording may add substantially to the general background knowledge and understanding of a given work, a composer, or an entire period in the history of music.

Travel to report on premieres and festivals in other cities and other countries  can be one of the benefits of the critic's work. It must be pointed out, though, lest too glamorous a picture be painted, that few publications have the budgets to support such junkets; it may more often be the industrious freelancer with arrangements to supply several different outlets with reports on the same event who does the traveling.

Until such time as recognized training programs for critics are established, enabling graduates to identify themselves as qualified with degrees or certificates, breaking into the field will remain primarily a matter of individual initiative and imagination.

Anyone interested in a career in criticism should investigate the training courses, seminars, institutes and workshops that are available from time to time. While the sponsors of these projects do not function as placement bureaus, it is the most direct way to come in contact with professionals of various levels, to register an impression with the senior participants and teaching fellows who may be in a position to make recommendations, and to hear about possible openings.


Richard Freed
Music Critics Association

# Careers in Communications

If you like music and also think you have writing skills, then you may want to consider combining them in one of the many jobs within the communications field.

Consider the many places you read about music: on record albums, in symphony programs, in advertisements for musical instruments, in newspaper and magazine articles, in the booklets that come with a new instrument you may buy. In fact, this entire book is about music.

Here are just a few of the related communications specialties in which you can use your musical knowledge:

**Publicity**— is the business of making certain that your client is well represented in the press, on radio and television. If you read a story in a newspaper or magazine about a musical group, for example, chances are that a publicist has been involved in making that story become a reality.

Publicists generally are responsible for preparing copy about their clients, making contact with the press and suggesting ideas for news and feature stories that deal favorably with the product, person or group they represent.

Most well known musicians employ publicists, and so do most record companies, as well as musical groups  and organizations.

Not everybody makes a good publicist: you need writing ability, a sense of creativity about what makes news and a good deal of personal integrity. And, you can't be afraid to call up people you don't know, establish rapport and present your story.

**Public Relations**—is a highly professional communications skill requiring in-depth knowledge of the subject you'll be working with, as well as all communications techniques and good business practice.

Public relations specialists employ publicity as one of their "tools," but they usually are involved in far-ranging efforts to develop a favorable image of their client. Musical instrument companies, music associations and educator groups are far more likely to employ public relations experts than people whose skill is limited to publicity.

Public relations specialists should be good, clear writers, and be able to write for several media (e.g., print, radio and television—as required), be able to research a problem and develop special events. Most important of all, they must understand the far-reaching consequences of communications challenges and be able to plan effectively to deal with them.

If you are interested in either publicity or public relations, your best training is writing. You may want to enroll in the journalism school of your college, or pursue a public relations curriculum which is now offered by some colleges and universities around the country.

However, if you can major in business, with a minor in journalism, you'll probably be best prepared for what will be required of you in a public relations career.

**Advertising**—is "selling" a company, its products, a musical organization or even one star personality through paid messages that appear in newspapers, magazines, on radio or television. To distinguish advertising from publicity remember that publicity appears in editorial space, whereas advertising is purchased. That means you have little to say about how publicity messages are interpreted and used by the press, whereas an advertisement appears exactly the way it was written and designed or produced.

Advertising work is handled both by independent agencies serving facets of the music business and by in-house staffs. That is, a company may maintain its own advertising and promotion department to prepare print ads and commercials. Often, companies employ a combination of the two.

If you seek a career in music advertising, the field is somewhat limited, and you would be better advised to plan for a broad enough education to handle any advertising chore rather than to focus entirely on music.

A college degree in marketing and advertising is highly recommended.

**Reporting** for newspapers, magazines, radio or television may involve covering community music events as news, writing about the music industry, interviewing musical stars, covering school music programs. (See also chapter on Careers in Music Criticism, page 115.)

Unless you are working for a trade journal that covers the music business exclusively, reporting for other media will mean covering events that go far beyond music.

You can begin to gain experience early by working on your high school or college paper, radio or television station. And, again, gaining experience in writing is the best way to develop the proficiency you will need to handle a professional job. A journalism major is recommended.

**Educational Materials** are a very important part of the communications effort by publishing firms and by musical instrument manufacturers. Both these fields need skilled writers who know a great deal about music. A writer involved in developing educational materials might prepare a brochure on flute playing techniques, might edit an entire magazine that goes to music educators or even author a book.

If you are interested in music education and writing, this area may present you with a very rewarding career. Your knowledge of music is of vital importance, but the ability to express your thoughts clearly and succinctly should also be developed through writing courses and through as many writing assignments as you can handle.

For any or all of these various career opportunities, you may want to start now to develop writing skills. Consider handling promotion or publicity for your school music group, or becoming a music reporter for the school paper. Offer your services to the community newspaper, or volunteer as publicity agent for a local band or orchestra.

The more practical experience you can bring to your first job, the more likely you are to land it. Remember that competition is strong and openings for the exact spot you want are limited. You may have to work your way up to the assignment you covet.

Opportunities as publicists are available in most cities around the country, but unless you find work in New York, Los Angeles or Chicago you may not be paid well enough to make this a full-time job.

Most public relations firms in the big three cities have music accounts, but don't forget that every symphony orchestra also needs publicity and public relations help, no matter where it is located.

The major music trade publications are also located in Chicago, New York and the Los Angeles area, but newspapers all over the country have general assignment reporters who may have music as their beat.

Advertising agencies draw their staffs from among writers who have gained experience in retail advertising, or working directly for individual companies or smaller agencies.

Public relations firms prefer writers with strong backgrounds on newspapers or magazines or with the electronic media.

And, some companies do hire beginners with exceptional talent or those who have gone through an internship connected with their college degree. Large newspapers hire students out of school, but if you want to get a sure start it's wise to work first on a small newspaper or magazine.

Research the firms with which you'd like to work. Read the music magazines, get to know what clients the advertising and public relations agencies represent and watch the kinds of things they do. Get to know people in the communications field. Join the student chapters of professional associations and attend meetings. You'll be able to find out more about the kinds of jobs available in the community, where the openings are and have access to job opportunities not generally known.

If the job you want is not immediately available, take one that will help you get to your ultimate goal. Always take advantage of opportunities to work with musical organizations on a volunteer basis and build up your sample case of music-related articles, ads or publicity.

Your perseverance, enthusiasm and natural talents will help you reach your career goal—communicating the enjoyment of music to others.

# Careers in Music Libraries

A music librarian is a specialist in music who works in a library. You are first a musician in the widest sense of the word, for music of any style, medium or era may find a place in a library, and you are also a librarian. Aptitude and training in both fields are necessary.

Music librarians work in several different kinds of libraries. Large music research libraries such as those at the Library of Congress or The New York Public Library employ a number of music librarians with comparatively specialized functions. These institutions serve a vast public and answer a wide variety of questions from complex research problems for musicological scholars to the location of obscure or out-of-print music for nationally known concert artists or for the man on the street. Librarians in these institutions acquire and integrate every kind of music and everything written about music into their enormous collections.

Most universities, conservatories and many colleges have separate music libraries with professional music librarians at their head. Such libraries usually offer research and reference facilities and circulating collections including scores and performing parts.

As music librarian you would work with the faculty to develop a library which will serve the needs of the students enrolled in courses and which will also provide more literature and information for the advanced or curious student. The librarian also cooperates with performing ensembles in the school, often helping orchestras, opera workshops or chamber ensembles to acquire the music they require.

Large public libraries in major cities frequently have either a separate music section or a combination music and art or performing arts section including dance and drama. Such libraries usually have large circulating record collections in addition to scores and books on music. Music librarians here need a wide knowledge of popular as well as serious music and must be particularly attuned to current happenings in the world of music.

Even smaller public libraries , which cannot employ a librarian to handle music exclusively , often have collections of circulating records requiring the supervision of someone with musical knowledge. Also public libraries often sponsor music recitals or festivals, or produce programs for local radio or TV. Here, as music librarian, you may find yourself acting as impresario or producer.

Certain special libraries also serve the music field. Radio and television stations may have their own libraries. Large music publishers and organizations like the American Society of Composers, Authors and Publishers sometimes hire music librarians to organize and deal with their holdings. Music dealers, too, often find library training valuable in their profession.

Orchestra librarians, whose main function is to acquire instrumental parts for an orchestra (usually by rental) and to prepare them for performance, occupy a somewhat special category in that they are not usually professional librarians. For this job, the ability to read and write music fluently and legibly is more important than the reference and cataloging skills used by other music librarians.

Since music libraries are comparatively small and specialized to begin with, as librarian you often have to assume several different functions—administrator, reference specialist, liaison with the public or faculty and the library staff.

Only the music cataloger is likely to work within a rather restricted sphere. The cataloger works comparatively alone, preparing catalog entries and subject headings and classifying new material according to the system used in a particular library. Cataloging can be an intellectually challenging task if there is a variety of material to be considered.

Outside of the large research libraries, most institutions do not employ more than two or three music librarians, with a cataloger and perhaps a recording specialist to assist the head music librarian. Salaries are not high. Although many music librarians earn enough to support a family, no one can ever become rich by working as one.

The field itself is not large and there is a consequent lack of mobility in the higher positions. Attractive openings are not always easy to find especially if geographical considerations are important. Most jobs are located in big cities and in college and university communities, but some of these, New York for example, are more popular than others. Even excellent qualifications do not guarantee the prospective music librarian the position he or she might prefer.

On the positive side, music librarianship can be consistently interesting to the intellectually curious person. Routine tasks are constantly varied by the changing needs of the library and its patrons. You have opportunities to be in contact with many areas and aspects of music. Within a few minutes you may shift your attention from a young flute student to a local opera director to a Japanese koto player or a teenage fan of country fiddling.

You are in a position to serve student and teacher, professional and amateur, composer and critic. Like many other people in the field of music, music librarians frequently engage in other musical activities in their spare time. Many music librarians are also performers, composers, critics and musicologists.

As librarianship is essentially an academic pursuit, intellectual curiosity and competence are requisites for success in the field. In addition, a librarian should have a good organizational mind.

Because people in the technical services connected with libraries, such as cataloging, often work behind the scenes, there are opportunities for shy or retiring types, but one should also recognize that most music librarians have to work well with people. A confident and outgoing personality is definitely an asset.

Perhaps the most telling sign that you are likely to be happy as a librarian is a deep love of books. Certainly a person who does not like books will not get the pleasure from being surrounded by them that most librarians feel.

Training for music librarianship should include as broad an education as possible in all aspects of music and the liberal arts supplemented by a year of graduate training in librarianship.

Curiously, most successful music librarians today did not choose this career early in their schooling. Probably this is because although the field itself is rather small, the background required is immense and only a student of varied interests is likely to accumulate the kind of knowledge a good music librarian needs to have.

For example, a music librarian needs a thorough knowledge of music history and of repertoire. In many positions a second master's degree (in addition to the library school master's) or a Ph.D. in musicology is required. Certainly graduate study including a thorough course in music bibliography is most desirable. Experience as a performing musician is also valuable. It gives the librarian practical experience in the requirements of many library users and acquaints him/her more intimately with a specific musical repertoire.

Since information about music and musical editions is likely to be published in any country and in any language, music librarians need a working knowledge of German and at least one Romance language to do the most basic cataloging or bibliographic research.

In addition to languages and the history and literature of music, the undergraduate should study a wide variety of liberal arts—history, literature, art and philosophy— because a music librarian needs to be able to draw on information and resources from other disciplines as well as his or her own specialty.

With all this knowledge to be accumulated, it is small wonder that formal training in librarianship usually comes rather late in the educational process. Most accredited schools of library science offer graduate programs of 30 or 36 credits culminating in M.A. or M.L.S. degrees, required for most professional jobs.

These programs offer training in the theory and practice of many aspects of librarianship, bibliography, reference, acquisition and cataloging, and administration. Some schools offer special courses in music librarianship or joint programs in music and librarianship. While these can be very valuable, you should be aware that there is no shortcut to acquiring the information a music librarian should have, and ultimately there is no substitute for quality.

If you think library work might be an interesting and satisfying career, as it certainly can be, the best way to find out is to work part-time in a library. Libraries usually have places for college and even high school students to help shelve books and perform minor clerical tasks. A knowledge of typing can help you advance at the clerical level, but simply being in and part of the library will acquaint you with many of its operations.

Hours are usually flexible; conditions are pleasant if you like books, and many students use the opportunity to earn extra money even if they have no plans to remain in library work. Practical experience working in a library can also be invaluable when and if you decide to go to library school by making the courses there more meaningful.

Susan T. Sommer
Music Library Assn.

# For Additional Information On:

## Allied Fields

Music Critics Association, Inc.
6201 Tuckerman Lane
Rockville, Md. 20852

The Music Library Assn.
343 South Main Street
Room 205
Ann Arbor, Mich. 48108

National Association for Music
Therapy, Inc.
P. O. Box 610
Lawrence, Kans. 66044

Society for Ethnomusicology
c/o Prof. Lois Anderson
School of Music
University of Wisconsin
Madison, Wisc. 53706

## Business

National Association of
Music Merchants
Suite 3320
35 East Wacker Drive
Chicago, Ill. 60601

National Music Publishers Assn.
110 East 59th Street
New York, N.Y. 10022

The Piano Technicians Guild,
Inc.
P. O. Box 1813
Seattle, Wash. 98111

## Education

College Band Directors
National Assn.
c/o University of California
Bands
59 Student Center
Berkeley, Calif. 94720

Music Educators
National Conference
1902 Association Drive
Reston, Va. 22091

National Association of Jazz
Educators
Box 724
Manhattan, Kans. 66502

National Band Assn.
Box 2454
West Lafayette, Ind. 47906

Women Band Directors
National Assn.
344 Overlook Drive
West Lafayette, Ind. 47906

## Performing Arts

Air Force Band
See your local Air Force recruiter

The American Symphony
Orchestra League
P. O. Box 66
Vienna, Va. 22180

Army Band
See your local Army recruiter

Operations Officer
U.S. Marine Band
Marine Barracks
8th and I Streets SE
Washington, D.C. 20390

The Navy Department
Music Branch
(PERS-724)
Washington, D.C. 20730

## Recording Industry

NARAS Institute
505 N. Lake Shore Drive
Chicago, Ill. 60611

Recording Industry Association
of America, Inc.
9200 Sunset Blvd.
Suite 1005
Los Angeles, Calif. 90069

Seven Arts Press, Inc.
(books, audio cassettes)
6605 Hollywood Blvd.
Los Angeles, Calif. 90028

# Suggested Periodical Reading

**American Music Teacher**
(Official Journal of the Music
Teachers National Assn.)
3587 S. Leisure World Blvd.
Silver Spring, Md. 20906

**Billboard**
One Astor Plaza
New York, N.Y. 10036

**Cash Box**
119 W. 57th St.
New York, N.Y. 10019

**The Choral Journal**
(Journal of the Choral
Directors Assn.)
P. O. Box 17736
Tampa, Fla. 33682

**Church Musicians**
(Publication of the Sunday
School Board of the Southern
Baptist Convention)
127 Ninth Ave.
Nashville, Tenn. 37203

**Clavier**
1418 Lake St.
Evanston, Ill. 60204

**Contemporary Keyboard**
Box 907
Saratoga, Calif. 95070

**Country Music**
475 Park Ave. South
New York, N.Y. 10016

**down beat**
222 W. Adams
Chicago, Ill. 60606

**Drum Corps World**
P. O. Box 130
Golden, Colo. 80401

**The Drumworld**
P. O. Box 1126
Radio City Station
New York, N.Y. 10019

**Guitar Player**
Box 615
Saratoga, Calif. 95070

**Hi Fidelity / Musical America**
The Publishing House
State Rd.
Great Barrington, Mass. 01230

**The Instrumentalist**
1418 Lake St.
Evanston, Ill 60204

**International Musician**
(Publication of the AFofM)
1500 Broadway
New York, N.Y. 10036

**Journal of Church Music**
2900 Queen Ln.
Philadelphia, Pa. 19129

**Journal of Music Therapy**
c/o National Association for
Music Therapy
P. O. Box 610
Lawrence, Kans. 66044

**Modern HiFi and Music**
699 Madison
New York, N.Y. 10021

**Musical Merchandise Review**
370 Lexington Ave.
New York, N.Y. 10017

**Music City News**
P. O. Box 975
Nashville, Tenn. 37202

**Music Educators Journal**
(Publication of the Music
Educators National
Conference)
1902 Association Drive
Reston, Va. 22091

**Music Journal**
370 Lexington Ave.
New York, N.Y. 10017

**Music Trades**
P. O. Box 432
80 West St.
Englewood, N.J. 07631

**NAJE Bulletin**
(Journal of the National
Association of Jazz Educators)
Box 724
Manhattan, Kans. 66502

**The Organist**
P. O. Box 4399
8432 Telegraph
Downey, Calif. 90241

**Percussionist**
(Publication of the Percussive
Arts Society)
130 Carol Dr.
Terre Haute, Ind. 47805

**Piano Technicians Journal**
P. O. Box 1813
Seattle, Wash. 98111

**PTM—The World of Music**
434 S. Wabash Ave.
Chicago, Ill. 60605

**Rolling Stone**
625 Third St.
San Francisco, Calif. 94107

**The School Musician**
P. O. Box 245
Joliet, Ill. 60434

**Stereo Review**
Ziff-Davis Publishing Co.
One Park Ave.
New York, N.Y. 10016

**Variety**
1400 N. Cahuenga Blvd.
Hollywood, Calif. 90028

**Woodwind World—
Brass & Percussion**
(For Professional Musicians:
Teachers and Performers)
17 Suncrest Terrace
Oneonta, N.Y. 13820

You may also want to review the
official publications of the
various state music education
associations; newsletters and
magazines published by individual manufacturers, as well as
newsletters and magazines
published by national and state
associations serving the career
areas of most interest to you.

Editorial supervision for
CAREERS IN MUSIC:
THE PUBLIC RELATIONS
BOARD, INC.

Graphic Design : The Niimi Design Group

# American Music Conference

*A Non Profit Organization Dedicated to Music*

**EXECUTIVE OFFICE**
3505 E. Kilgore Rd., Kalamazoo, Mich. 49002
616/344-1697

**PUBLIC RELATIONS**
150 E. Huron, Chicago, Ill. 60611
312/266-7200 or 312/649-0050